# THE MAKING OF BRITAIN

## The Dark Ages

# THE MAKING OF BRITAIN

## The Dark Ages


edited by

Lesley M. Smith

MACMILLAN

To Mary and John Smith



First published 1984

Published by
Higher and Further Education Division
MACMILLAN PUBLISHERS LTD
Houndmills, Basingstoke, Hampshire RG21 2XS
and London
Companies and representatives
throughout the world
Typeset and designed by Columns of Reading
Printed in England by
Pindar Print Limited, Scarborough, North Yorkshire.

British Library Cataloguing in Publication Data
The Making of Britain.
The Dark Ages.
1. Great Britain — History
I. Smith, Lesley
941 DA30
ISBN 0-333-37513-0
ISBN 0-333-37514-9 Pbk

# Contents


| | | |
|---|---|---|
| | List of Maps and Illustrations | vii |
| | Acknowledgements | ix |
| | Preface | xi |
| | Introduction<br>*Lesley M. Smith* | 1 |
| 1 | A Continent in Ferment<br>*Philip Dixon* | 7 |
| 2 | After the Romans<br>*Malcolm Todd* | 21 |
| 3 | The Anglo-Saxon Migrations<br>*Richard Hodges* | 35 |
| 4 | The Emergence of Anglo-Saxon Kingdoms<br>*Patrick Wormald* | 49 |
| 5 | Picts, Scots and Britons<br>*Wendy Davies* | 63 |
| 6 | The Christian Connection<br>*Liam de Paor* | 77 |
| 7 | The Viking Nation<br>*Klavs Randsborg* | 91 |
| 8 | The Vikings in Britain<br>*Alfred P. Smyth* | 105 |
| 9 | One English Nation<br>*Pauline Stafford* | 117 |

10 The Kingdom of the Scots
*A.A.M. Duncan* 131

11 Myths of the Dark Ages
*Janet L. Nelson* 145

12 The Feudal Kingdoms of Europe
*Philip Dixon* 159

Notes 173

Notes on Contributors 185

Index 187

# List of Maps and Illustrations


1. The Western and Eastern Roman Empires 8
2. The route of the Goths to the Roman Empire 10
3. The Forum at Rome 13
4. The Villa Tivoli 14
5. The distribution of barbarian tribes outside the Empire 15
6. A typical German settlement 16
7. Barbarian grave goods 17
8. Barbarian metalwork 18
9. The threats to the Roman province of Britain 22
10. Chedworth Roman Villa 24
11. Mosaic from Lullingstone Roman Villa 25
12. A mosaic depicting Christ, from Hinton St Mary 26
13. The threefold threat to the Western Roman Empire 28
14. Reconstruction of Wroxeter, early fourth-century example of a Roman town 29
15. The baths at Bath 31
16. Trade between German barbarians and the Rhine provinces 16
17. Roman glassware from a barbarian burial 37
18. The Nydam Ship 40
19. Carved ship prow 41
20. Anglo-Saxon settlement in Sussex 43
21. The reconstructed Anglo-Saxon village at West Stow, Suffolk 43
22. Anglo-Saxon grave goods from Winterbourne Gunner 45
23. The kingdoms of Britain c.597 50
24. The Anglo-Saxon kingdoms c.825 51
25. Offa's gold dinar 52

26. Offa's silver penny 52
27, 28, 29. Treasures from the Sutton Hoo ship burial 54-5
30. The distribution of royal vills known from pre-conquest sources 57
31. Charter of King Aethelbald 'Rex Britanniae' 61
32. The distribution of languages in Celtic Britain 66
33. The Ivybridge Stone 67
34. The Irish migration to Scotland 68
35. The British kingdoms 69
36. The fortress of Dunadd 71
37, 38. Legal records copied into the Lichfeld Gospels 73
39. Pictish symbol stone 74
40. Tintagel 79
41. The evangelisation of Ireland 79
42. Skelling Rock 81
43. Skelling Monastery 81
44. Iona 83
45. Celtic crosses on Iona 86
46. A page from the Book of Lindisfarne 89
47. The Ruthwell Cross 89
48. Viking trade routes 92
49. The Gokstad ship 93
50. The fortified wall and harbour at Birka 96
51. Ornate cup from Jelling 97
52. The Jelling Stone 99
53. Jelling 99
54. The Trelleborg Fortress 100
55. Viking raiders 104
56. The Viking invasion of Britain 106
57. Silver penny of S Edmund 111
58. Viking tombs from York Minster 112
59. Stone depicting a snake pit 112
60, 61, 62, 63. Silver pennies of Cnut, Guthrum, Gothfrithsson and Eric Bloodaxe 113
64. 'One King under one God' 118
65. Silver penny showing Edgar as king 119
66. Document showing Edgar as king 119
67. The division of England on Watling Street 121
68. Stone Anglo-Scandinavian tombs 121
69. The King with his ealdormen 123
70. Edgar flanked by his archbishops 128
71. The peoples of Scotland 130
72. The Aberlemno Kirkyard Stone 132
73. A Scottish kinglist 133

74. Hilltop sites 134
75. Sueno's Stone 138
76. A page from the Book of Kells 142
77. A page from the Book of Deer 143
78. Queen Victoria and Prince Albert depicted as a Saxon king and queen in the Mausoleum, Frogmore 148
79. Victorian representation of Alfred inciting his troops to victory 149
80. Manuscript showing peasants at work 151
81. Manuscript showing nobles feasting 152
82. Manuscript showing the condition of women in Anglo-Saxon Britain 155
83. Alfred's contribution to British naval development: a Victorian view 156
84. Silver penny of Alfred 157
85. The Frankish Empire 160
86. Model of the palace complex at Aachen 161
87. Charlemagne 162
88. The Viking invasion of Normandy 163
89. Mounted soldiers 165
90. King Canute 169
91. William's army at Hastings 170

The publishers wish to acknowledge the following illustration sources:

Barnaby's Picture Library 3, 4, 10, 15, 91; Mr Ray Gardiner 25, 26, 57, 60, 61, 62, 63, 65, 84; The Schleswig-Holstein Landesmuseum 7, 8, 18; Bridgeman Art Library 11; Trustees of the British Museum 12, 19, 27, 28, 29, 55; The Castle Museum, Shrewsbury 14; The Danish National Museum 17, 51, 52, 53; West Stow Anglo-Saxon Village Trust 21; Salisbury and South Wiltshire Museum 22; The Lodonek Press 33; Mr Mick Sharp 36, 40; The Dean and Chapter of Lichfield Cathedral 37, 38; Anna and Graham Ritchie 39; The Office of Public Works, Dublin 42, 43; Mr Ian Fisher 44, 45; Janet and Colin Bord 47; Oslo University Museum of Antiquities 49; Dr Bjorn Ambrosiani 50; Mr T. Balslev 54; Mr S. Croad 58; The Werner Forman Archive 59; The British Library 46, 64, 66, 69, 70, 80, 81, 82; Mr Peter Saabor 68; The Mansell Collection 89; Trinity College Library, Dublin 76; The Lord Chamberlain's Office 78; The Department of the Environment 75, 79.

The publishers wish to state that every effort has been made to trace all the copyright holders but if any have been inadvertently overlooked they will be pleased to make the necessary arrangement at the first opportunity.

# Preface

This book is based on the television series *The Making of Britain* made by London Weekend Television for Channel Four. I am very grateful for all the help I received from those at London Weekend Television who developed and produced the series – Barry Cox, David Tereshchuk, David Coulter and Mike Flood Page. My thanks are due also to the individual contributors who shared with me their knowledge and enthusiasm for the subject, and saved me from errors of interpretation both in the book and in the series. A number of other scholars in the fields of archaeology and early medieval history also advised me and I should like to thank in particular Bertil Almgren, Nicholas Brooks, James Campbell, Tania Dickinson, David Dumville, Simon Keynes, Peter Salway and Martin Welch. Sarah Mahaffy proved a sympathetic and most helpful editor, especially in the later stages of editing. Finally, Debbie Hall, Pam Wilkinson and Jane Crush typed a difficult manuscript with great patience.

L.M.S.

London, February 1984

# Introduction

Lesley M. Smith

The making of Britain is a process with no discernible beginning. Any starting point is arbitrary and at first sight the confused centuries between the fall of the Roman Empire in the early years of the fifth century and the Norman invasion of England in 1066 seem an unlikely place to start. For over six hundred years wave after wave of alien invaders – Angles, Saxons, Jutes, Scots from Ireland, Norwegians, Danes and French-speaking Normans – swept across England, Scotland and Wales; attacking, if not always conquering, indigenous populations, and overturning, if not always destroying, existing political, economic and social structures.

Yet beneath this troubled surface something very interesting was happening. The nations of England, Scotland and Wales emerged with something akin to their modern borders. And the languages we speak, Welsh and Gaelic as well as English, were first used and, more important, written down in forms still recognisable today. Although neither historians nor archaeologists can yet explain why, the outlines of modern Britain were clearly fixed during those Dark Ages.

Despite its popularity, the 'Dark Ages' is something of a misnomer. It reflects the feeling of older generations of historians that there was no virtue in the societies that succeeded the glorious Roman Empire. The violence, instability and paganism of these kingdoms and the terror struck into the hearts of civilised Christian monks by the later Viking raids seemed to indicate that along with the Roman Empire fell all trace of civilisation. Spiritual and cultural darkness, they believed, spread over Europe and civilisation was not to reappear in any permanent form until the dynamic papacy of the eleventh century initiated the revival of learning and religious faith that took final shape in the twelfth century renaissance.

This view reflects the prejudice of an orderly, centralised, literate and above all deeply Christian society, rather than any profound historical truth. It also reflects the special difficulty faced by historians who study the Dark Ages: documentary evidence about even the most important people in early medieval society – the kings and their nobles – is at best sparse and frequently non-existent. Evidence about other classes in society even now poses problems of interpretation that fill academic journals and conference halls with acrimonious debate. We know far more about the Roman Empire and the later Middle Ages than we know about this crucial era in Britain's history. J.A. Giles wrote in 1861 of the Germanic invasion of England in the fifth century: 'But of this great revolution, the most important our country has ever suffered, we know almost nothing.' Despite over a century of endeavour which has clarified the progress of this migration, and the origins of those who participated in it, we know little more than Giles did about why it actually took place, or why it proved successful. Although these centuries are no less 'dark' than tradition proclaims, it is the darkness of ignorance, not barbarism that has clouded the view of the historian.

Nevertheless, the last hundred and fifty years have seen enormous steps forward in the reassessment of the Dark Ages. To many scholars, particularly archaeologists, John Kemble is the father of that scientific approach to the study of the early medieval period which has been responsible for the most spectacular advances in our knowledge.

Kemble lived in the first half of the nineteenth century. After a brief burst of revolutionary ardour that led him to fight in the Spanish revolution of 1830, he settled down to take his MA at Cambridge. Two years after he graduated, he expounded his view of England's origins in a series of impromptu lectures largely attended, a colleague records, by fellow Trinity men anxious that he should not want for an audience. He contended that scholars should work with the earliest sources at their disposal: to do that they needed a better understanding of the Anglo-Saxon language and a willingness to study artefacts and sites of settlements. As the ancestors of the English came from Germany, they had to be studied there, as well as in England. These views brought him considerable scorn from colleagues. He was accused of falling under the dangerous sway of misguided German literati. Not content with absorbing this knowledge, he then committed the ultimate sin of applying it to the past, thus robbing Englishmen of their distinctive heritage. In the outraged words of one adversary: '. . . we have no longer Anglo-Saxon, but German Saxon.' The academic establishment, then as now, could stand only so much novelty.

Kemble survived this onslaught to become a scholar with an international reputation. By 1849, when he published his magisterial survey *The Saxons in England*, he was a member of learned scientific societies in half a dozen European capitals. Ironically, but perhaps not surprisingly, he was not elected to similar honours in Britain. He died in Dublin in 1855, after an academic career devoted to mastering any discipline, including philology and archaeology, that could help to explain England's origins.

His approach (which today might be termed interdisciplinary) harnessed the antiquarian studies of his predecessors and contemporaries into a much more systematic study of history. Within twenty years of his death his methods and conclusions had been accepted and history, including the history of the so-called Dark Ages, had become an expanding discipline in British universities. Cosmo Innes, Professor of History at the University of Edinburgh, summarised contemporary attitudes when he advised his students to go directly to the original sources for their study and to forget the 'twice-told tale of the historians of the bookshelf'. He went so far as to propound the view that they should avoid even the elegant summary of David Hume (one of Edinburgh's leading scholars of the Enlightenment), and use instead the rough and vivid picture presented by contemporary chroniclers. When he came to tackle the early history of Scotland, Innes began with an assessment of Charlemagne and his influence on the early medieval world, recognising the importance to Britain of events in Europe. Under the direction of like-minded teachers, history began to move out of the gentleman's library and into the archive and archaeological 'dig'.

By the beginning of the twentieth century, the preoccupations of scholars had changed once more. For example, in 1906, T.W. Shore wrote that his aim was not to describe the conquest of England by the north Germans and Scandinavians, but to analyse the settlement of England by the conquering tribes and races. He was looking for farms and villages, not the sites of battles; the houses and streets of these settlements, not the routes and progress of armies. This interest in people and their everyday lives, rather than kings and their battles, has increased in recent years. Insights borrowed from anthropology and sociology have been applied to societies that are distant in time, not place, enabling archaeologists and historians to reconstruct the daily life of many of these settlements and to present a picture of the rituals and mores of their societies.

These developments are just one strand in the historiography of the Dark Ages. But they do prove beyond doubt that history is an active process, constantly evolving under the impact of new evidence, new techniques and new perspectives. It is this process that we have tried to illuminate in this book. The contributors all challenge accepted ideas and relate their own specialised research to the central question of why Britain emerged in a recognisable shape during those turbulent centuries.

The twelve chapters run chronologically from the destruction of the

Roman Empire to William of Normandy's invasion of England. They emphasise that Britain was first and foremost part of a wider world in which events far distant from this island could have a dramatic effect on our history. Philip Dixon shows how the population migrations that triggered the collapse of the Empire with special consequences for Britain in comparison with the rest of Europe, had their origins far away on the steppes of Russia, or, in some cases, on the eastern borders of China.

Richard Hodges and Klavs Randsborg both use the concept of an integrated world economy to unite disparate archaeological and historical data into an explanation of two major invasions of Britain – by the Angles and Saxons in the fifth and sixth centuries, and by the Norwegians and Danes in the ninth century. In each case there is a parallel process of trade collapsing under stress, leading to raid and settlement in each case. Klavs Randsborg further qualifies the Viking invasion of Britain by pointing out that it was just one incident in a spectacular Scandinavian expansion stretching, at its zenith, from the Caspian Sea to the eastern coast of North America.

Britain is more than just England, although the anglo-centric bias of much historical writing has ensured that we know more about England than about the other nations of Britain. Malcolm Todd discusses the British contribution to life in England after the Romans abandoned the province, while Wendy Davies explains convincingly how the north and west of Britain, largely unconquered by either Romans or Anglo-Saxons, preserved a diversity of culture and social organisation that not only formed the basis for present-day Scotland and Wales but also influenced the later development of English society. A.A.M. Duncan concludes this story by reassessing the fascinating process whereby a small band of Irish migrants, the Scots, gave their name and language to most of the lands north of the Tweed. Liam de Paor traces three distinct missions to Christianise Britain; of these, the mission of the Celtic Church, based in Ireland and western Scotland, was hardly less influential than the mission sent from Rome by Pope Gregory the Great.

One of the most creative developments in early medieval history is the application of novel techniques and new perspectives to familiar evidence. Richard Hodges applies methods drawn from anthropology to the analysis of the latest archaeological discoveries. He reconstructs the political and social structure of Germanic society to explain why the Angles and Saxons were so successful as colonists when they reached England. Patrick Wormald approaches some of the most traditional evidence about the Dark Ages – royal charters and the Anglo-Saxon poem *Beowulf* – from a standpoint that allows him to describe the lives of the king and his warriors in terms of the relation between this elite and the ordinary people whose labours made their luxurious life-style possible. Alfred P. Smyth and Pauline Stafford take a later period and show how the settlement of Danish invaders in the north and east of England merely reinforced existing northern hostility to the southern kingdom of Wessex, at this time represented by Alfred the Great and his descendants. Far from being a patriotic victory over Scandinavian invaders, the union of England under this dynasty was much more the successful conclusion of a long-standing policy of southern expansion.

At the time of the Norman invasion, which was yet another conquest of north by south, the outlines of modern Britain are recognisable. Perhaps for this reason, these centuries have been a source of self-definition for Britain, and have produced some of the most potent myths of nationhood that we possess. Janet Nelson shows how historians and writers since the twelfth century have used their visions of the Dark Ages as a standard against which they can measure their own age. By investigating these myths, she sheds light on the way we understand our own past and, in doing so, reveals the process by which history is made.

The writing of history is a perilous exercise, and this book may well enshrine some myths of its own. However, in introducing the history of the Dark Ages, we have tried to convey some of the excitement of historical research while at the same time indicating just how difficult and, occasionally, arbitrary the practice of history can be. Each generation reinterprets the same events (such as the Viking invasions or Alfred's defeat of the Danes) in the light of its own experience and preconceptions and, ultimately, history is not made by great men, natural disasters or impersonal economic trends – it is made by historians themselves.

CHAPTER ONE

# A Continent in Ferment

## Philip Dixon

Britain is a small island at the extreme northwest of the continent of Europe, protected by a narrow channel from the mainland, and often insulated from the political and cultural upheavals that have disturbed Europe throughout its recorded history. At the dawn of this period, over two thousand years ago, three great empires stretched across Asia and Europe. The Chinese Empire survived until the twentieth century; the ancient kingdom of the Persians was absorbed by the Arabs in the seventh century AD; and the youngest, the Roman Empire, fell victim in the fourth and fifth centuries AD to internal pressure and barbarian invasions, which eventually brought to Britain settlers from North Germany and Scandinavia.

In recent years scholars have given increasing emphasis to those elements of British life that remained intact for thousands of years, a continuity in farming and settlement which was indifferent to the political dominance of Celtic chieftains, Roman governors or Anglo-Saxon kings. But the end of Roman power marks a real change in the history of Europe, for the flood of German conquerors ushered in a new age for our remote part of the empire, an age of isolation which saw the gradual evolution of the nations we recognise today as England, Scotland and Wales.

In AD350, more than half of Europe lay within the Roman Empire, and had done so for over three hundred years – a span of time equivalent to the period from the English Civil War to the present day. The empire was divided for administration into two halves, the West and the East, but it had a unified currency, and a common language, Latin. It had a regular army stationed across the provinces to maintain peace; a complex network of roads, way stations and military bases; and a highly organised bureaucracy and tax system. Above all, it united the lands around the Mediterranean into a single entity: men

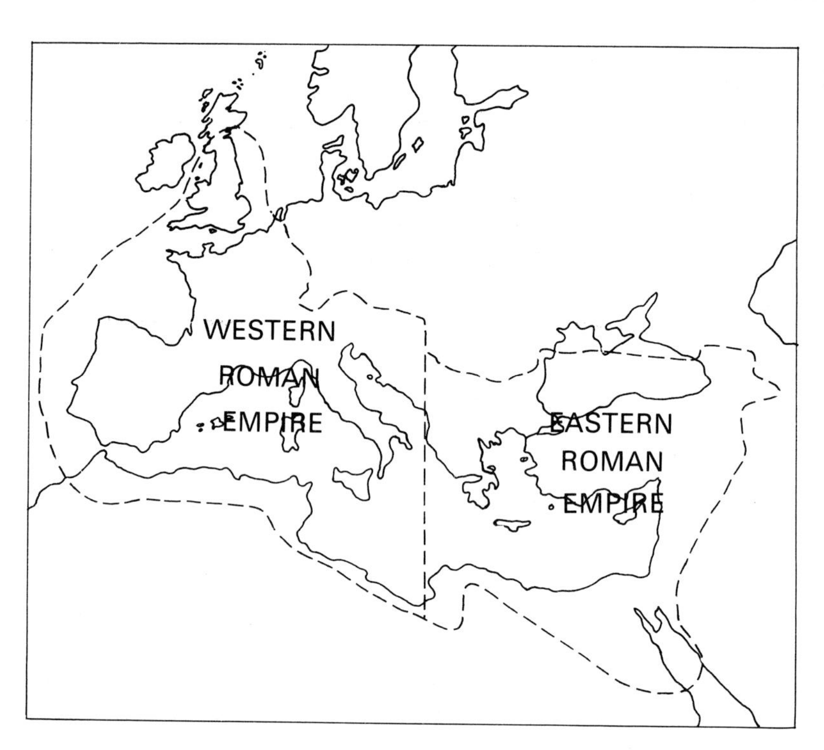


1. The Western and Eastern Roman Empires

moved freely around this area and, wherever they went, found familiar art and religion, familiar town-planning, familiar clothing and class structure. The rich travelled most freely, the poor not at all. But in between were many thousands of men in the army, the civil service and the church, whose duties took them from one side of the Roman world to another. An imperial edict could bring together a cavalryman from Syria and a general from Spain, and send them to Britain, where they might find an African from Carthage or even an allied German king on military service with his retinue.[1]

Beyond the frontiers of the empire, especially to the north, Roman writers pictured moors, marshes and vast dark forests, peopled by fearsome German tribes. Romans generally tended to call them *Barbari*, barbarians, a half contemptuous reference to the sound of their incomprehensible languages: 'ba, ba, ba'. Beyond this, few Romans had more than a passing interest in them, and a study of their travellers' tall tales gives us only a poor idea of the real nature of the northerners.[2]

Yet in the middle of the fourth century, these barbarian kingdoms stretched from the south Russian steppe to the Dutch coast, the entire length of the imperial frontier in Europe. Some tribes were large, others were small; most were restless and footloose. They were all German-speaking and a man from the Russian Crimea could probably make himself understood in Scandinavia. Due to their destructiveness, the names of some have been resurrected for modern use – Hunnic atrocities, Vandal outrages and Gothic horror stories. Others gave their names to the areas where they eventually settled down: the Burgundians in southern France, the Lombards in Italy, the Franks in France and the Angles in England.

All along the frontier the barbarians indulged in border raids. From time to time, usually when Roman forces were for some reason dispersed, a border raid could turn into a serious threat to the empire. But after each incursion, Roman troops rebuilt the defences and restored the status quo, with some changes – for example, a district might be tacitly ceded to the raiders, or some country houses would be left in ruins and abandoned.

This pattern of Germanic pressure and Roman counter-pressure was well established by AD370. The situation was suddenly transformed by the westward migration from the Russian steppes of a race of nomads new to Europe, the Huns. Surprisingly little is known about these notorious people. Descriptions of them emphasise their flat noses, small eyes and lack of facial hair – characteristics we now call Mongol – and it may be that some of them at least had crossed Asia from the Chinese border. Their first victims were the Gothic kingdoms to the north and east of the river Danube, the frontier of the Roman Empire. In two or three campaigning seasons, they conquered and absorbed these kingdoms and in 376 drove a large number of refugees to the imperial frontier.

The commanders of the Roman forces defending the frontier took little notice of the rumours of distant battles until the refugees began to gather on the river bank, asking for permission to cross into the empire. The numbers of refugees increased; trying to count them, said a contemporary writer, was like counting the sands on the shore of Lybia. The Emperor Valens, far away in Syria, decided that these newcomers would be useful recruits for the imperial armies, and the starving Goths were allowed to cross under the control of the local garrisons.[3] Disorganisation provoked a disaster, for the Goths had no food, and the Romans little provision for helping them. In a fashion familiar to all ages the newcomers fell victim to the extortion of profiteers; they sold their children into slavery to purchase dog meat. They were now both numerous and angry, and the Roman troops could no longer check them as they spread into the fertile lands of Thrace. When Valens led an army to keep them away from the imperial capital of Constantinople he was killed and his army routed; his successor allowed the Goths to take the Danube lands under their own control, with their own laws and rulers.

Although the Huns had been the catalysts for this incursion, they themselves occupied the ancient Gothic lands outside the empire and

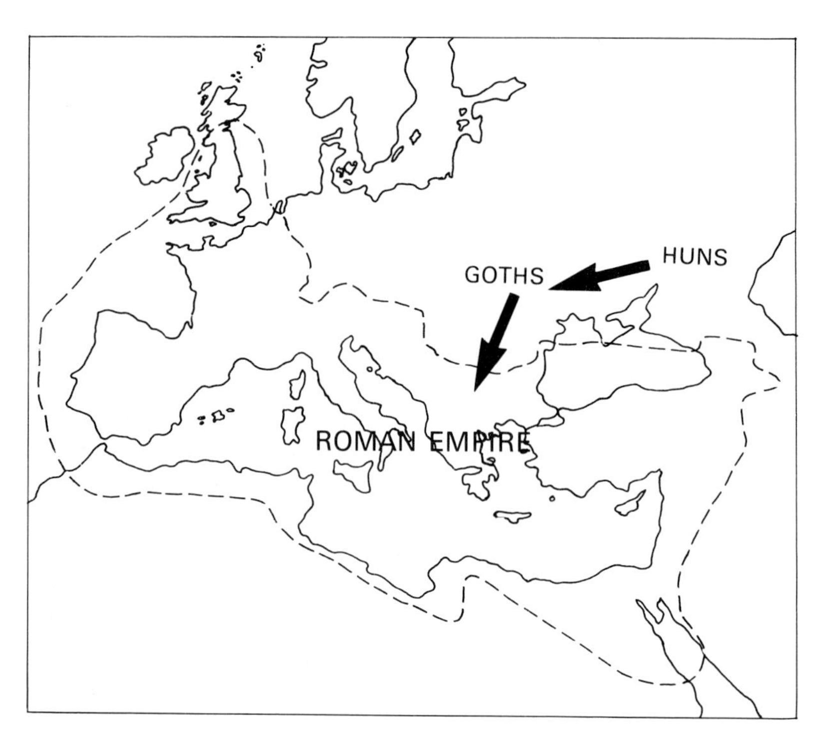


2. The route of the Goths to the Roman Empire

presented no immediate threat to Rome. Indeed, many were to be found serving as mercenaries in Roman service. The real threat came from the German border tribes, who may have been dislodged by pressure from the Russian steppes, but more likely saw Roman confusion as an opportunity for plunder. More and more troops were withdrawn from the frontier to defend Italy from invaders, and in the early years of the fifth century these pressures combined to bring about the collapse of the Western Empire.

The Goths had proved uncomfortable neighbours and were by now based in Jugoslavia, as far from Constantinople as they could be encouraged to go. Their leader, Alaric, like all barbarian chieftains, was anxious either to forage for plunder or to be paid to stay away. When the western government refused to buy him off, he marched to the Italian frontier, hoping to force agreement to his demands. At this time, the end of AD406, the Rhine frontiers were also breached by a motley army of local German tribes who passed westwards towards the Channel and, over the next three years, crossed France and went south into Spain. Meanwhile the Roman troops in Britain, alarmed by the indifference or inability of the imperial government to stem this advance which effectively threatened their links with the continent, rebelled and crossed the Channel. Their leader, Constantine, set up a rival empire based at Arles in southern France. Alaric invaded Italy, where he sacked Rome in 410; he then went pillaging in the south with the aim of crossing to the rich corn lands of Africa, the El Dorado of several barbarian peoples. The outcome was significant: despite their pillaging and burning the barbarian invaders were tolerated and even enrolled to assist the imperial government. The government's chief fear was of an internal enemy: not the Germans, whose violence could be harnessed, but the rebels who threatened to upset the imperial system. With Gothic help, the kingdom of Arles was crushed and the British and Gallic rebels dispersed.[4]

By 420 some stability returned to Europe, but the changes were striking. Britain, no longer part of the empire, drifted first into the hands of the rebels and then into those of the provincial oligarchies. Spain was largely out of control, dominated by Vandals and Alans. They then invaded Africa where they dealt a death blow to Mediterranean trade by capturing the great port of Carthage and the rich corn lands that had long provided food for Italy. Gaul was split between the Goths (settled around Bordeaux), the Franks (who had insinuated themselves into Belgium and the north of France) and the Gallo-Roman provincials under the great general Aetius. For thirty years Aetius maintained a precarious balance of power in Gaul, moving a tribe here, decimating another there, negotiating with the Goths and with the Italian government – for Italy, in effect, was all that was left of the Western Empire.

These changes continued. Aetius was assassinated in 455, soon after his triumphant defeat of the first (and last) Hun invasion of the Western Empire, under the greatest Hunnic king, Attila. With Aetius gone, the status quo disintegrated. There was little to stop the Franks from moving south and the Goths from moving north until they met at the end of the 480s, and established their common border on the Loire. Weakened by attacks of Vandals from Africa, Italy fell victim to a small Ostrogothic army, recently ejected from the Eastern Empire. This, indeed, was general collapse and smaller tribes grasped the opportunity to spread into neighbouring lands; the Burgundians moved into the valley of the Rhône, and the Angles and Saxons travelled into Frisia and Belgium, and across the North Sea into the eastern parts of Britain.[5]

The pattern of the Dark Ages – small barbarian tribes constantly at war with one another – had now been set. But throughout all this, the Eastern Empire survived, its boundaries now shrunken. Its Greek orthodox religion increasingly distinguished it from the West. Its foreign policy seldom ranged beyond the Balkans and Anatolia. But for the German kings whose ancestors had dismembered the West it remained a powerful reminder of the universal Roman Empire, something for them to imitate even in the unlikely milieu of their fortified palaces in the forests and mountains of Germany.[6]

This short account of the barbarian catastrophe provides no immediate explanation of why the Roman Empire fell. The empire was a network of interdependent societies and economies, and changes and calamities in one part caused decline and disruption in another. No single explanation can account for the way in which this great complex ground to a halt, but this has not stopped commentators from making free with their opinions. Each generation has provided reasons that appeal to its own prejudices. In the fifth century, the church fathers feared that the fall was due to the state of sin of the empire – it was the just retribution of God. In the eighteenth century, Edward Gibbon, who was irritated by the irrationality and illiberality of religion, wondered how much of the catastrophe was due to the debilitating effects on the morale of society caused by the early Christian Church itself. Scholars of our own age, in some ways less credulous, have turned their attention to our own preoccupations: the economy and social injustice.

There are three main lines of explanation. First, the empire was growing weaker because of internal problems; some form of break-up might have been expected in the West, even without the final barbarian attacks which perhaps only hastened a process already under way. Second, the frontier line was too long and too hard to defend without draining resources from the land to maintain a large army. Even measures such as the division of the empire into an eastern and western half for administrative purposes could not solve the problem. Finally, the nature of barbarian attacks was changing and becoming more insistent, so the empire was forced to keep increasing the strength of its responses. Each of these theories has some truth in it.

Before the empire collapsed it fell into decay. One theory holds that the exploitation of slaves caused the downfall of Roman civilisation. But all the civilisations of the ancient world were based on slavery, as were those vigorous German successors of the empire, which used slaves until the thirteenth century at least. However, it may be true that heavy land taxes and the exactions of landlords turned sturdy peasant farmers into bondsmen, limiting their economic freedom and mobility and thus weakening the labour market and the army. Certainly there were signs that the low level of military recruitment was causing concern, and towards the end of this era even captured barbarian tribes were drafted into the army. In some areas too, civic duties, which were time consuming and expensive, were being shirked by the traditional ruling class. In addition to this depressing picture, shrinking population might have accelerated the decline.[7] The model can be made to work, but the evidence is very thin.

In particular, the area often cited as typical of the decay, the Middle

3. The Forum at Rome

East, maintained a thriving town and country life, as good an indicator of economic and political health as any. Towns, with their markets and industries, provided a crucial part of the economy, and only when they declined was that economy in trouble. But in western Europe this was exactly what happened. A number of towns, for example, Autun, Nimes and Beauvais in France, collapsed and were rebuilt on so small a scale that they are best seen as forts or the citadels of local notables, and not real towns at all. Though excavations have told us less about the countryside, it is beginning to be clear that the shrinking of these towns reflected a general decline in these areas.[8]

The focal points of the Roman countryside were the villas, the country houses of the wealthy, where agricultural produce from the great estates was collected and sent into the towns. In Germany, in northern Gaul and along the Danube frontier, many villas were in decline after the 260s, when most of that area was ravaged by local German tribes. Although there are signs of regrowth, they are few and it seems likely that these regions were slowly decaying. When the sustained invasions came in the late fourth century, they were thus less able to recover than they had been a century earlier.[9]

4. The Villa Tivoli

Even in prosperous times the frontier itself was ill-suited to prolonged attack. Quite apart from the frontiers of Africa, Anatolia and the Middle East, all areas that needed constant attention, the frontier of the empire in Europe was enormous. From the Rhine estuary to the mouth of the Danube it ran for more than two thousand kilometres, often leaving the tactical advantage to the enemy. The roads made communication rapid, in ancient terms; it could still take over a fortnight for news to pass from one end to the other. By the time of the final breakdown, the military danger inherent in this situation had been acknowledged. The troops stationed actually on the frontier had been reduced in strength, and were now intended only to delay enemy attack. The main forces were pulled back to the interior of the provinces, to places where the road network was conveniently sited for rapid deployment to relieve the frontier troops. It was a bold strategy, but it could not cope with concerted efforts and simultaneous attacks over a wide front. Soon after the year 400, as more and more units were brought back to Italy, a military disaster became almost inevitable.

However, this disaster did not affect the whole Roman world, as we have already seen. The size and the growing complexity of the empire had, for fifty years, made it sensible to spread the administration between two governments and two co-emperors, based in Constantinople in the east and Ravenna (instead of Rome) in the west. Although this was a sensible scheme it actually increased the problems, for the two bureaucracies frequently failed to act in unison,

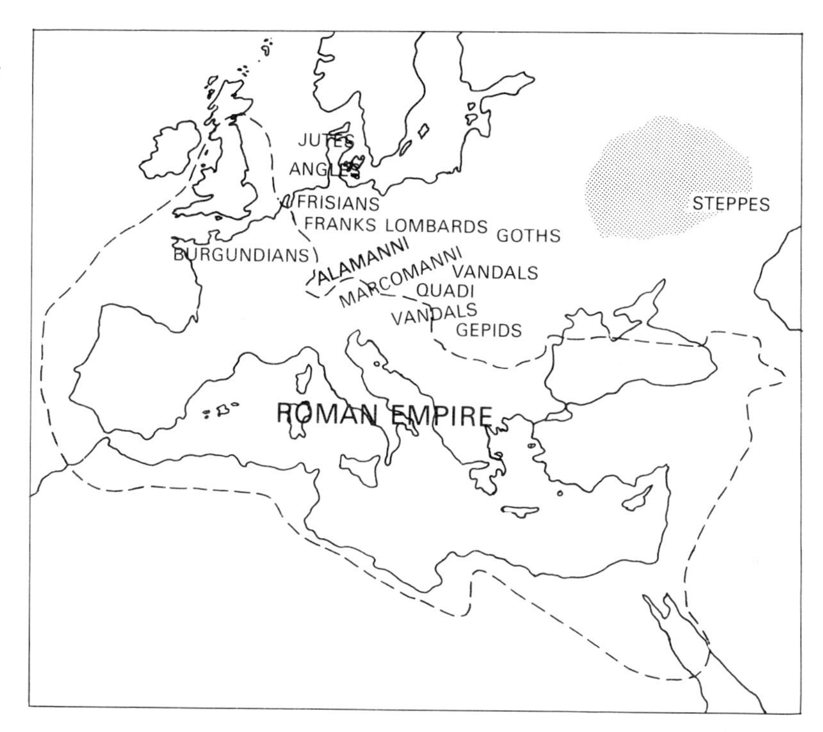


5. The distribution of barbarian tribes outside the Empire

and the temptation to encourage dangerous allies to seek their fortune in the other half of the empire was sometimes overwhelming. Twice in the fifth century Italy was conquered by Goths from Jugoslavia who had been encouraged on their way by the government of Constantinople.

The Eastern Empire was often in danger. It too suffered from the Goths and later from Attila and his Huns, but its frontier in Europe was short and could be defended easily. Its resources – its fertile lands – lay outside Europe in Anatolia and the Middle East. As long as the threat came from Europe, from the Germans and the Asiatic nomads, Constantinople remained secure.

But western Roman failures – lack of unity and economic and social decline – are only half the story; the other half is the growing sophistication of the barbarians themselves. In the early days of the empire, Rome's opponents were badly organised, small tribal groups, which frequently squabbled with each other. Opposition to Rome brought them together, and we begin to hear of larger and larger groups, dangerous confederations with specially devised names to indicate their new status: Marcomanni (marchmen or borderers), Alamanni (allmen or union), Franki (freemen), or Picti (tattooed men). These were the Romans' real enemies.

Written sources tell us little about the internal affairs of these Germans, for they left no records of their own. But archaeology does tell us something about their way of life. They had no towns, and even their largest settlements were no more than villages. Apart from a very few specialists, they were farmers by trade and warriors when required. Their houses, outbuildings and barns were built of timber and twisted wattles, covered in mud and thatch. In the majority of cases, the farmhouses lay in small clusters in the middle of their fields, surrounded by moors, waste and woodland.[10]

Amid this age-old pattern of life, however, things were changing. In the two or three centuries before the migrations, the level of population was rising. For example, the Dutch settlement of Wijster expanded from a couple of farmsteads to a regularly planned village of thirty or forty houses linked by streets and separated by boundary fences.[11] Similar developments can be traced in sites along the north German coast.

The excavation of cemeteries also tells us the same story of rising populations. In the first century AD most settlements were very small, with few burials. During the third and fourth centuries, burials were frequent as the population expanded. In the fifth century there comes a sudden end to burial, and the majority of the graveyards were abandoned as the migration south and west into the empire began.

6. A typical German settlement

7. Barbarian grave goods

But some movement is clear before this time. In the early years (AD100-250), there is little variety in the style of pottery in the burials. New fashions become common in the late third and fourth centuries, and the diversity is considerable. In north Germany, in particular, Danish-style pottery became popular, indicating possible migrations from Jutland to the North Sea coast, migrations which exacerbated population pressures and created the culturally mixed federations in the years before the great invasions.[12]

Archaeology shows the results of German attacks. We can see the evidence first in the peat bogs of Jutland, which contain huge ritual deposits of weapons and other valuables as offerings to the tribal gods of fertility and warfare. A large proportion of the offerings are of Roman manufacture, the gods' share of the Germans' booty.[13] Barbarian metalwork of the fifth century shows a sudden and striking skill. Along with the plunder, Roman craftsmen must have been carried off into Germany to create these new fashions. The settlement sites of the north German coast and Jutland were, almost without exception, abandoned in the fifth century, and a gap of over a century separates these sites from the new foundations of the seventh century

8. Barbarian metalwork

and later. After a rapid rise in population from 250 to 400 we have a virtual abandonment of the ancient homelands.[14]

Why did these Germans go to the trouble of uprooting their households? To get plunder, of course, and the Roman weapons and armour dedicated to the gods of the peat bogs show how common the prestigious practice of plunder had always been. Through much of the late fourth century raiding parties were probing the strength of the frontier. Some probably knew of the empire from the Roman traders whose goods (glass, metal and pottery) have been found in Germany and Scandinavia.[15] Others may themselves have once served in the Roman army and learned how attenuated were the empire's defences, and what profits could be made in the Roman world. But these were essentially Germans who robbed and returned home again.[16]

Much more interesting, and eventually more destructive to Roman civilisation, were the barbarians who entered the empire and settled there. They were looking for land, but they also wanted to join the empire. They wanted a share in its prosperity, not to destroy it. They sought prestige, comfort, wealth and all the benefits of civilisation. In short, they wanted to become Roman noblemen, not Roman peasants. The traditional stories of fire, sword and pillage bear little relation to the careful legality with which the conquerors were allocated specific estates, acquired the boundaries to their property and shared the revenues with the former Roman proprietors (who may themselves have done no more than hand over the state land tax to the resident barbarians).[17]

The Gothic kings imitated Roman customs and lost no time in codifying their ancestral laws in Roman fashion. Indeed, the Gothic leader, Athaulf, went so far as to marry Galla Placida, the sister of the Western Emperor, a formidable lady who subsequently became dowager empress-regent of Italy. Later, the Goths of Italy, through Roman propagandists, attempted to harmonise Roman and Goth into a single state, with considerable attention to formality and protocol. Even the more barbarous Franks, a frontier people further from the civilisation of the Mediterranean, produced a pastiche of *Romanitas*, the essence of being a Roman. But the very presence of these independent kingdoms hastened the break-up of the old empire. The dislocation caused by their arrival, the new customs and the new politics, eventually ended in the disappearance of the prosperous Roman state they hoped to join.[18]

The newcomers everywhere must have formed only a fraction of the community. A recent estimate puts the whole German population before the migration as low as two or three million against a Roman army in Europe of about a quarter of a million, and a total population of the empire in Europe of perhaps twenty or thirty million.[19] The Germanic successor kings conquered in battle; they did not swamp and evict the indigenous peoples. Thanks not least to the speed of conquest, they took over the political system, the social hierarchy, the Christian religion and the local industries of the Roman Empire with little alteration. The changes and the slow dwindling of *Romanitas* took generations.

During these years, the wars and migrations continued. For a time, indeed, the eastern government, vigorous and expansionist under the Emperor Justinian, recaptured Africa, Italy and part of Spain. The result, however, was merely to increase the fragmentation. The Lombards and other German peoples soon moved in, and the holy wars started after 630 by the Arabs, successors of Mohammed, gave the government in Constantinople quite enough to worry about on its eastern borders without further adventures in the west.[20] In the consequent power vacuum, Italy fell into that state of disunity and disorder in which it remained throughout the Middle Ages. Spain, part Gothic and part Arab, was a battleground until the fifteenth century. Central and eastern Europe fell victim in the seventh and ninth centuries to new waves of Asiatic nomads, the Bulgars and the Magyars, while northern Europe, after a brief revival as a would-be empire under the Frankish king, Charlemagne, was torn by internal rivalries and ravaged by Scandinavian pirates.

Roman power in Europe largely disappeared in the fifth century AD, and the majority of Roman institutions had effectively vanished by the eighth century. Almost all that survived was a memory of former unity and an aim, expressed by Charlemagne on the edge of his seal: 'The Renewal of the Roman Empire'.

## Further reading

P.W. Dixon, *Barbarian Europe* (Oxford, 1976); A.H.M. Jones, *The Later Roman Empire* (Oxford, 1964); M. Todd, *The Northern Barbarians* (London, 1975); J.M. Wallace-Hadrill, *The Barbarian West* (London, 1967).

CHAPTER TWO

# After the Romans

Malcolm Todd

On the face of it, there would seem to be few more decisive breaks in British history than that which marks the end of Roman rule in Britain. For three and a half centuries, Britain had been part of the Roman Empire, garrisoned by a Roman army, administered by imperial officials, paying its dues to Caesar and enjoying, for at least some of that long period, the fruits of the Roman peace. At one moment Britain was still part of that empire; the next she was severed from it, cast adrift and at the mercy of barbarian forces who came to plunder her wealth and to throttle civilised life. The potent (and false) image of the last Roman troops embarking on their ships and sailing off to the defence of Italy still haunts the popular imagination. Was the break really so sharp? What led up to it? What was the state of Britain after the end of Roman rule but before the invasions of the barbarians which began in earnest about fifty years later?[1]

For more than half a century before the final abandonment of Britain, the western part of the empire faced serious problems both on its frontiers as barbarian attacks were stepped up, and internally as ambitious commanders sought to grab whatever fleeting power was still there for the taking. Like the other western provinces, Britain came under increasing barbarian threat and at the same time saw more and more of her armed strength drained away to serve in power struggles on the Continent. By 400, the military position of Britain was parlous and the end was not long in coming.

By a curious chance we know as much about the events leading up to the ending of Roman rule in Britain as about any period of Romano-British history after the late first century, and a good deal more than we know about the years immediately before it occurred, a fact which has not always received full recognition.[2] We owe this knowledge to an account of events in Western Europe from 406 to

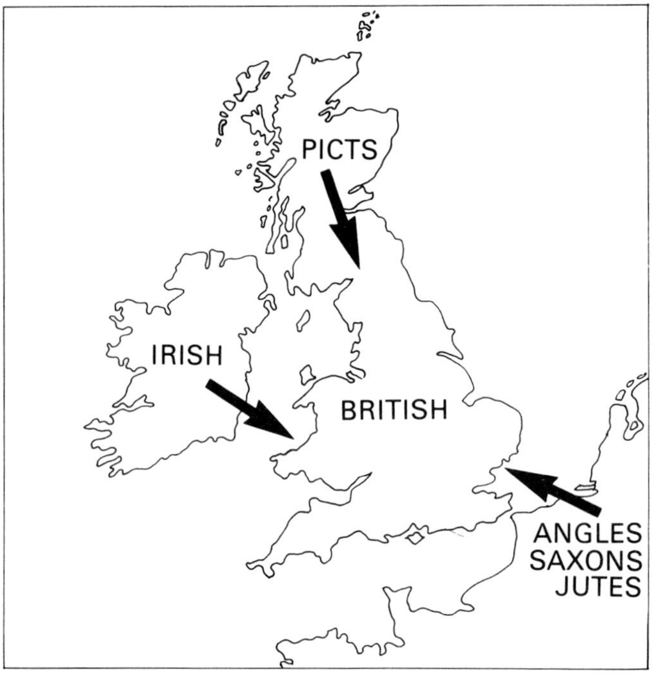

9. The threats to the Roman province of Britain

409 from the pen of Zosimos, a Greek writer living about AD500. On the last day of 406, a vast army of barbarians crossed the frozen Rhine and moved westwards towards the Channel coast. It began to appear as though Britain might be invaded and the forces of Britain were seriously alarmed. Earlier in the year they had elevated an otherwise unknown soldier, Marcus, to supreme power. He had not lasted long, being supplanted at the time of the barbarian advance through Gaul by Gratian, an urban magistrate or councillor. Gratian survived for only four months, the army's next choice falling on another soldier, Constantine, commonly known as Constantine III. No doubt the army thought that his leadership might save Britain from the barbarians. That the army remaining in the island had the power to do pretty much as it pleased is nakedly apparent; there is no sign of any effective control being exercised by a Roman commander with allegiance to any emperor. Very soon after his elevation, Constantine crossed to Gaul taking a considerable part of the army with him, and over the next eighteen months he was able to extend control over much of the Roman West. Left to look to their own defence, and realising that they could no longer expect help from Constantine or his army, the Britons took up arms and freed their cities from the attacks of barbarians from across the sea. Zosimos is quite explicit about what the Britons did. They rebelled against Rome

and removed themselves from Roman jurisdiction. This is an unusually clear account. Can we believe it?

No one would rank Zosimos among the best historians of the ancient world. It is easier to make a case for him being one of the worst. But in this section of his work he is following the account of a writer of a far different calibre, the great Olympiodorus, who was living at the time when these events in the western provinces took place. What can be said with confidence about Zosimos' story is that it is entirely credible and coherent. It is not the kind of thing that he, or anyone else, is likely to have invented, even if he were capable of anything so original. Constantine III left the Britons on their own, without adequate protection, and they responded by taking matters into their own hands.

The break with Rome was intended to be total. What Zosimos does not tell us is who the motive force behind the revolt was. This is important as it might indicate who took power in Britain when the collapse of Roman authority was complete. It is sometimes assumed that this was a movement of the poor and landless against their masters, as was the revolt in Armorica, the western part of Gaul, a few years later. There the rebels expelled the Roman officials and promulgated a new constitution. But if that were so in Britain, it is odd that an immediate objective of the Britons was to rescue their cities from barbarian attack. That action is more comprehensible if the rebellion was headed by members of the urban oligarchy and other landowners who had most to lose if the urban centres fell. The reaction was natural enough. The power of Rome, or what remained of it, had failed them. Why should they continue to contribute money and men to the empire and receive nothing in return?

There was no attempt by any emperor or commander to restore Britain to Roman rule after 409. In the following year, the feeble emperor Honorius is reported to have written to the cities of Britain telling them (or allowing them) to take measures for their own defence.[3] All he was doing was covering the fact that the British communities had already acted on their own behalf. Honorius was simply closing the file on Britain.

What was this corner of the empire like before it broke free from the grasp of Rome? Although it was a troublesome province in the first and second centuries, by the early fourth century Roman Britain was enjoying her most prosperous phase.[4] Ironically, it was perhaps Britain's isolation from the Continent that accounted for this prosperity. For example, the province was far from the frontier in Germany where, late in the third century, barbarians not only threatened but breached the imperial defences, to the lasting detriment of many areas. In fact, Britain's agriculture – the principal source of

10. Chedworth Roman villa

wealth in the Roman world – was now at its peak, regularly exporting a large surplus to the Rhineland; her borders were secure, her population at its height. The southern and central parts of Britain were studded with cities and smaller townships linked by the best communications Britain enjoyed until the eighteenth century.

Wealth in the Roman Empire meant land and some of the landowners of late Roman Britain were wealthy indeed. Like the gentlemen of Georgian England, they displayed their wealth in fine country residences such as Chedworth and Woodchester. These pleasant seats were the centres of working estates, staffed by slaves and local peasant workers. Nevertheless, they could still be adorned with sculptures and splendid wall-paintings and mosaics, often depicting vivid scenes from pagan mythology. They also had bath suites and elegant gardens. In the early fourth century, many villas were enlarged by their owners, and new building was undertaken all over Britain, most particularly in the Cotswolds. Rural life was obviously both profitable and secure.

11. Mosaic from Lullingstone Roman villa

From these great estates were dispatched the food supplies necessary to maintain life in the cities. In effect, the cities were linked with the countryside by the closest economic and social ties, for the men who ran and administered the cities were the same men who owned the large agricultural estates.[5] Rome had always depended upon the willingness of native landowners to take their share in the burdens of empire, and this might include providing major amenities for a city, such as public baths, temples, the water supply, even parts of the defences. In the early years of the empire such provision by private individuals had been easy to organise. By the fourth century, as the burdens of taxation and tribute pressed ever more heavily upon communities and individuals alike, the ability and the willingness of provincial peoples to maintain these urban amenities at the earlier level was no longer so marked. All the same, the towns of late Roman Britain were still lively places. As the plan of Silchester in the Thames Valley shows, towns were not heavily built-up and the population of each was usually only a few thousand. Most of the inhabitants were

12. A mosaic depicting Christ, from Hinton St Mary

engaged in agriculture or associated trades such as smithing, tanning and textile-making. Some luxury trades existed. Traces of a large silversmith's workshop have been found in Silchester, while in York and Lincoln Gaulish merchants were busy buying and selling wine. There would also be those who furnished the necessities of day-to-day life, such as bakers, and masons to build and decorate the town houses of the rich, and repair public buildings. However, little in the way of large-scale industry was conducted in the city.

Most towns still boasted public squares, a forum where shops could be rented by individual traders, or stalls erected on market day. There were well-planned streets, a piped water supply and, in a few places such as Lincoln, excellently constructed sewers. Recreation was not neglected: as well as taverns and bars, pagan temples and smaller shrines, there were small amphitheatres in a few towns where citizens might watch a gladiatorial contest, bear-baiting or even the death of criminals. All were safe places, ringed with strong defences.

Religious expression was very varied in the fourth century. The traditional Roman gods still had their temples and their followers. Native Celtic cults were still alive and in the more remote areas may have remained so until the close of Roman Britain. Other gods had been imported from the eastern provinces of the empire, or even beyond, as in the case of the Persian god, Mithras.[6] Formally, however, from the early fourth century Britain like the rest of the empire was a Christian land. The faith had made major progress among the upper levels of society by the late fourth century, although few churches have yet been discovered.[7] An example at Silchester is one of the few known instances of an urban church. Some villa owners had their own private places of worship, like that at Lullingstone in Kent, with its fine frescoes showing Christians at prayer. Another house-church in the villa at Hinton St Mary in Dorset had a fine mosaic floor dominated by a central picture of a young man with the Chi-Rho monogram behind his head, the Greek letters Chi and Rho forming the first two letters of the name of Christ himself. Probably this is the earliest-known image of Christ in Britain.

The early Christians in Britain were neither poor nor isolated. The silver treasure found recently at Water Newton near Peterborough includes several objects that are plainly liturgical vessels; they must surely have come from a church and were perhaps buried at a time of crisis. One of the most important features of this treasure is the fact that a few objects are inscribed with phrases and lines of verse which are reminiscent of usages current in the eastern provinces of the empire, suggesting that British society was in touch with currents of ideas and art which flowed far and from many sources.

Although Romano-British society was peaceful and outwardly prosperous, there was a weakness: its intellectual inspiration, in so far as we can judge, was limited and came from far-off lands and far-off days. No notable writers or thinkers are known to have originated in the island, with the exception of the heretic Pelagius and St Patrick. This void may have helped to undermine the strength of society when it faced its severe tests in the fifth century. More important for Britain was the fact that it depended almost totally on Rome for administration and defence. The dangers inherent in this dependence grew steadily more apparent as the future of this Romano-British way of life was threatened by the concentration of imperial resources on the defence of the heart of the empire, more than one thousand five hundred kilometres away.

From this point, the security of Britain came under increasing threat. We hear of barbarian raids of great scale, in 360 and 364 and, in 367, a major invasion from across the North Sea and from the Picts and Scots to the north and west.[8] The next crisis which Britain faced came in 383, when the military commander of the island, Magnus Maximus, revolted against the authority of Rome, trusting to his popularity with the army for support. Maximus was not slow to extend his authority over the neighbouring province of Gaul, and because he took a sizeable army with him his action must have led to a reorganisation of the forces left behind in Britain. The military garrison in the island was clearly reduced after Maximus' seizure of

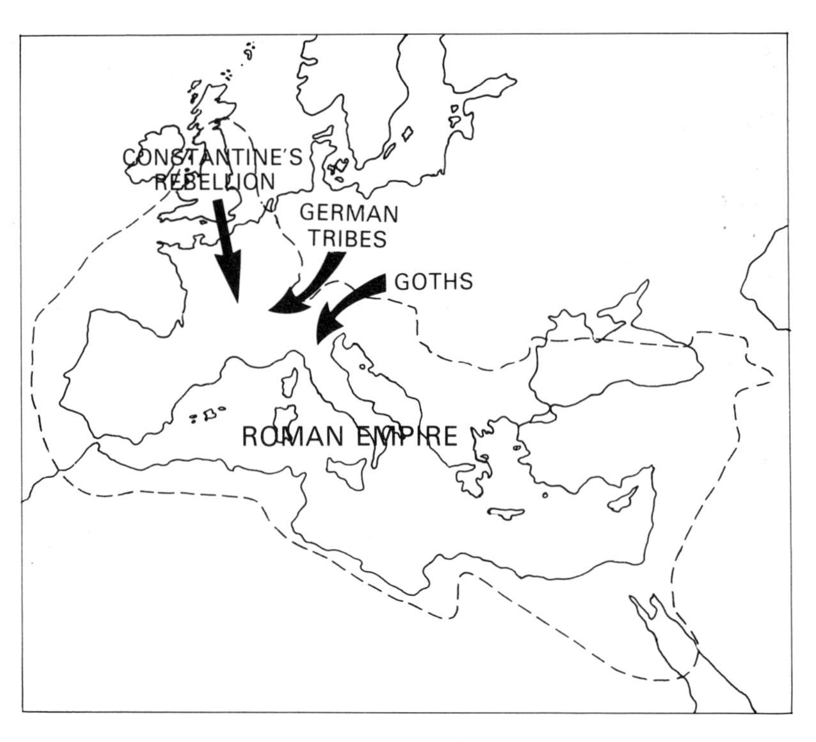


13. The threefold threat to the Western Roman Empire

power and after he fell, in 388, there is no sign that it received any strengthening. For example, many of the forts in the western Pennines and North Wales were never reoccupied, creating a serious weakness in Britain's defences. Shortly before 400, Britain again had to be rescued from her barbarian foes, this time by the most powerful general of the Western Empire, Stilicho. Stilicho's intervention was the last occasion on which a major expedition was mounted against the enemies of Britain; soon after the situation had been retrieved, Roman forces in the island were further reduced to serve in Italy against the invading Goths. By 401, Britain's military strength had been largely drained away and Constantine's expedition to Gaul in 407 completed the process. Hereafter, we can find British regiments serving in Europe, and even in the East, but apart from the small garrisons which probably remained in some of the walled towns the island itself was left undefended.

After the abandonment of Britain, there were bound to be rapid and far-reaching changes. The relationship between the Romano-British aristocracy, which had administered the cities and their territories, and the imperial government was a thing of the past. What took its place? No doubt there were many local and regional variations, but it seems probable that the surviving British land-owning families tried to hold on to their power. For a time, many of them may have succeeded. But

14. Reconstruction of Wroxeter, early fourth century example of a Roman town

the absence of a central authority in Britain would have worked against the local magnates in the long run. The evils of Roman taxation had gone, but so had the protective umbrella of Roman power. Without the central administration to organise the sophisticated economic bases of Romano-British society, the fabric of that world began to decline.

With less demand from the towns and garrisons, the great agricultural estates became isolated, unsure of a market for their produce and, perhaps in the years of barbarian raids, unable to plant or harvest crops. It must also have been difficult in such unsettled conditions to maintain the necessary work-force on the estates. But judging from the evidence available, it seems likely that there was at first only a gradual decay in the rural economy, rather than a sudden and abrupt cessation of cultivation across the province. The same is true of the towns and cities. In the circumstances of the early fifth century, it is not surprising that people continued to live within their protective walls. But although these were still centres of population, it is unlikely that they survived as anything more than the nuclei of purely local power.

The picture that is presented of the cities of southern Britain in the fifth century is not uniform. Here decay and ruin, much as the sixth century writer Gildas describes, is the order of the day; there continuity of settlement is clearly evident, at least until about the year 500. This is, of course, to be expected. The major barbarian raids and settlement came in the south and east, and only slowly did the invaders expand into the west and north of Britain. In these western parts of Britain we might reasonably expect to see signs of continuing urban life well after 400, and such indications are present. At Wroxeter, near Shrewsbury, a large area near the centre of the city was replanned and rebuilt, in timber not stone, in the fifth century, and the community here could well have survived until well into the following century.[9] At Exeter, too, although there are clear signs of dereliction in the late fourth century, some of the public buildings were being partially restored at the end of the Roman period.[10] Although some of the towns and cities may have been too large for the requirements of the social order now beginning to emerge, many continued to be inhabited. Indeed, both Cirencester and Gloucester housed British communities until the sixth century, as the ninth century *Anglo-Saxon Chronicle* reveals. Possibly some of the smaller walled townships such as Bath were more attractive centres for fifth and sixth century communities. Another literary work of the ninth century tells of a hot lake where men may bathe and much later there is mention of a roofing vault still in place over the spring. Some of the larger cities, however, still retained a population.[11] At Verulamium, buildings were still going up in the mid-fifth century, and a piped water-supply was laid on even later.

It was not just the remnants of Romano-British society that sought shelter in the towns. Where urban decay is apparent, for example at Canterbury and Dorchester-on-Thames, early Anglo-Saxon houses were located within the walls of the Roman towns. It is also known that the dead were buried within the walls, and at Canterbury, Anglo-Saxon jewellery has been found in these graves. This evidence is beginning to suggest that barbarian communities may have given new life to these settlements after the end of Roman rule. Their function, however, had changed. These towns and cities were no longer connected by a network of trade and administration: they were individual units, surviving as well as they could in a countryside that must have seemed increasingly hostile.

Turning now to the centralised industries, these appear to have

15. The baths at Bath

collapsed in the early years of the fifth century. Some, including major potteries and metalworking centres, were winding down or ending before 400. With the slackening of urban and military demand, the markets on which they had depended for so long were no longer there, or had contracted so far that centralised manufacture was no longer required. Furthermore, the successful distribution of goods could only take place if there was a well-organised system of transport and guaranteed order in the country. This is not to say that all crafts came to an end. There is good evidence that pottery-making and metalworking continued on a local basis until well into the fifth century, and other crafts which leave little trace behind them, such as textile manufacture, are also likely to have been maintained.

No more compelling indicator of the collapse of economic life can be singled out than the fate of the coinage. For three and a half centuries coinage had been a normal feature of life in Britain, serving the needs of the population and, above all, allowing troops their pay and the tax-collector his due. Gold coins, mainly from the mint in Milan, were still reaching Britain in quantity between 380 and 400. There were still abundant silver coins in circulation, and we must not forget that Britain herself may have been producing some of the silver bullion for the western mints even at this late date. In 400, then, coinage was still performing a role in the economic system. Within a decade that role had been largely lost. After 402 the flow of gold and silver into Britain was checked, mainly because there were no longer large numbers of Roman troops to be paid. Small numbers of coins entered in the following years but by 425 at the latest coinage had come to an end and it was not to be revived until the origins of Anglo-Saxon gold coinage in the seventh century.

The events of 406-9 do seem to mark a decisive break in the history of Britain. Before 406 the island manifestly belonged to the Roman world. After 409 its fate was undecided, but outside the control of Rome. Yet the break came only as the culmination of processes that had been undermining Romano-British society for several decades. Thereafter, social structures which were fundamentally Celtic or British reasserted themselves. In the east of Britain these were quickly overlaid by Anglo-Saxon society. In the west and north, Celtic structures were to survive for centuries. In the highland areas, where the essential structures of Celtic society survived intact beneath the imperial wrapping, local potentates may now have been able to take advantage of the removal of Roman authority and establish themselves as the masters of miniature kingdoms not far removed from the kingdoms of pre-Roman days.[12] Some of these British magnates aspired to greater authority, in one or two cases over much or all of what had been Roman Britain. The first of these may have been the 'proud' or 'supreme' tyrant, whom Bede calls Vortigern, who brought an Anglo-Saxon warrior-band into Britain to support his position. There is evidence from the very earliest traces of barbarian settlement in southern Britain that Vortigern tried to follow the example of the imperial authorities when faced with barbarian attack. He hired barbarian mercenaries to defend his territories, settling them permanently on good land in return for their services. Because the barbarians whom he employed quickly turned against him and established their own control over Kent where they were settled, Vortigern has generally been treated harshly by historians. But he was doing no more than Roman emperors had been doing for well over a century. His error was to ignore the fact that times had changed.

The 'British dimension' in fifth century history has received far less attention than it deserves, chiefly because the available literary sources give greater prominence to the Anglo-Saxon advance in the east and the south than to the substantial survival of the Romano-Britons. Archaeology, too, has more to offer on the material culture of the newcomers – their metalwork, pottery, burials and settlements – than on the fading culture of the British.

However, the Britons were there – as certain classes of place-names containing the element 'wealh' (i.e. Celts, British) clearly reveal – and we cannot really understand what happened in the fifth century without assessing the British contribution of the period. Even at the end of the century about half of Britain was still under British control and much of the west was to remain so throughout the sixth century. Some areas were in contact with the Roman world in the late fifth century.[13] It might be more accurate to say that they had re-established contact after a break of some decades. Fine tableware from the eastern Mediterranean world and from western Gaul was reaching settlements in the south-west of Britain, Wales, western Scotland and Ireland in the years immediately before 500. Containers of wine and oil travelled the same routes westward to enliven the feasts of British lords and, it may be guessed, for ecclesiastical use. There were other contacts, of which we have only hints, between the south-west, Ireland, Brittany and Merovingian Gaul in about the year 500. Also, relations with the Germanic rulers of eastern and southern Britain may not always have been as hostile as the *Anglo-Saxon Chronicle* suggests.

Roman rule in Britain ended in the early years of the fifth century, but all sense of Britain as part, albeit now a detached part, of a larger world in which Rome was still a considerable power was not immediately lost. Latin remained the language of learning and civilised converse. For Gildas in the sixth century it was still *nostra lingua*. A large part of Britain was still a Christian land after severance from the empire and the Christian faith was not the least of the legacies of Roman Britain. But henceforward Britain stood naked and unprotected, beyond the limits of the world of Rome, vulnerable to barbarians on all her shores and with no champion able to rise to her defence.

## Further reading

L. Alcock, *Arthur's Britain* (London, 1971); S.S. Frere, *Britannia. A History of Roman Britain* (London, 1978); C. Thomas, *Christianity in Roman Britain* (London, 1981); E.A. Thompson, 'Britain, AD406-10', *Britannia* VIII, pp. 303-18 (1977); M. Todd, *Roman Britain* (London, 1981).

CHAPTER THREE

# The Anglo-Saxon Migrations

**Richard Hodges**

> From that time Britain, or the British part of it, which had been stripped of all its armed men, its military supplies, and the whole flower of its active youth . . . lay wholly exposed to plunderers. . . .[1]

With these words the Venerable Bede, writing in 731, two centuries after the event, noted the beginnings of the Anglo-Saxon migrations. The migrations, of course, were one episode in the epic events of fifth century Europe. Entire communities were uprooting themselves at this time and setting out in search of more prosperous or at least more satisfactory homelands. As the Roman Empire became focused upon the Mediterranean, barbarian tribes such as the Alamanni, the Burgundians, the Franks and the Visigoths transformed the political and ethnic configurations of north-western Europe.[2]

Britain was abandoned by the Roman legions in the early fifth century, after more than three centuries of colonial rule. This left a power vacuum into which two peoples looked ready to move: in the north and west were the Celtic peoples of Scotland and Ireland, the Irish and the Picts; in the south, Germanic barbarians 'from the three most formidable races of Germany, the Saxons, Angles and Jutes' (according to Bede) were poised to invade areas they had previously attacked. Two centuries later, these barbarians controlled practically all the south and east of the country, carving out numerous kingdoms that were to become the nucleus of Anglo-Saxon England. These barbarians were the ancestors of the English and played a central role in the making of Britain. But where did they come from? Why did they come to Britain, and why were the Anglo-Saxons – as opposed to the Celts who lived nearer – able to achieve so much?

We shall never know the real answer to these questions. Historians of the time have told us too little, and the archaeological remains cannot be stretched towards reconstructing the precise sequence of events. Even so, we can hazard some calculated guesses which can be tested as more sites are found and excavated by archaeologists. But before doing this, let us first consider the political and economic context of these Germanic tribes before they came to Britain.

The Angles, Saxons and Jutes lived in a world which was very different to that of the Roman Empire which they helped to destroy. In the empire there existed a complex society ranging from a labouring class to a middle class, to bureaucrats, a professional military elite and, of course, an aristocracy. There were state-run industries and, by the fourth century, large state-run farms. The Roman world was complex in every sense and governed by laws debated in the senate as opposed to traditional tribal codes. Moreover, in Roman society as in our own the eldest son tended to inherit his father's wealth and to maintain the family's lineage. By contrast, Germanic and Celtic society was far less complex, though hardly barbaric. These tribal communities constituted the Third World during Roman times and, as in our modern world, their political organisation was rather different to the state-run machinery of the

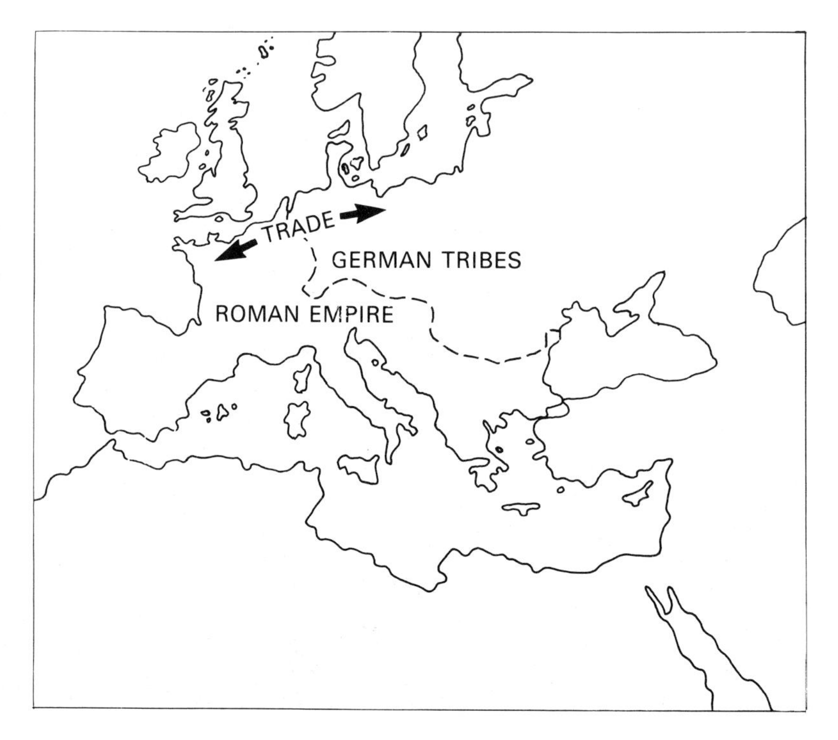


16. Trade between German barbarians and the Rhine provinces

empire. Anglo-Saxon society was principally an agrarian way of life: everyone lived in villages. Specialised groups simply did not exist in any significant number: there were no labourers, no entrepreneurs and no bureaucrats. In addition, relationships within these tribal communities were principally founded upon kinship rather than upon law codes reinforced by the state.

Celtic and German society in the fourth and fifth centuries appears to have been a ranked or chiefdom society. The office of the leader – the chief or king – is the essence of this political arrangement. He was elected and supported by the principal families (lineages) in the community. Indeed, he was the paramount figure, but his actions were closely monitored by the nobility so he was rarely able to secure the succession of another member of his family. He was restricted by social conventions in other ways as well. To go to war, for example, he had to raise a militia from the community as there was no professional army in a society of this kind. In these circumstances the support of the leading families was vital if a war was imminent. In fact, to construct or plan anything within his chiefdom required

17. Roman glassware from a barbarian burial

authority to do it. This authority might be generated, however, by carefully controlling the economy. In particular, long-distance trade with a rich alien state might provide prestige objects sufficient to impress the community, and capable of reinforcing the chief's position.[3] In the Roman period, for example, the German chiefs received glassware, fine pottery vessels and a variety of jewels from Rhenish traders who were based in Roman towns such as Bonn, Cologne and Mainz.

To the ordinary Anglian, Saxon or Jutish peasants these objects were invested with a mysterious quality belonging to a remote and sophisticated civilisation. To possess these imported goods was a symbol of prowess and alliances which added up to power. The chief might give away a good proportion of these imported goods as gifts, often in a lavish and conspicuous display of generosity at weddings, funerals or other religious festivals. Nonetheless, the position of such a leader could be easily threatened in a crisis brought about by defeat in war, environmental catastrophes or simply the cessation of the trade connection supplying the prestigious goods.

The Celtic and Anglo-Saxon territories, in practice, had very different political systems. The power of Germanic kings was much more considerable than that of their Celtic counterparts. Moreover, an aristocracy appears to have existed in German society, exercising considerable influence on royal trade relations with the Romans. Wealth in this community, however, was passed on to one's next of kin, or at most divided equally within the family. However, in the Celtic kingdoms tradition demanded the equal division of a man's patrimony amongst his family. The inevitable result was a patchwork quilt of tiny territories. The accumulation of immense wealth by one man was prevented by the inheritance system. To complicate matters further, from the late fifth century onwards the newly founded Irish Church began to acquire a large amount of secular property, thereby delimiting the potential authority of any Irish chieftains. Significantly, German chiefs were not to experience this partition of their power-base until they adopted Christianity in the seventh century.

Now we know what the Anglo-Saxon and Celtic societies were like, we must begin to examine the reasons for the migrations. First, we have to look back two centuries. By about AD200 certain north German tribes had established firm relations with Roman traders. Consequently, when the empire began to suffer a period of intense inflation and subsequent recession, so too did the Angles, Saxons and Jutes feel the cold winds of economic change. The parallel with modern times, with the impact of the recession on Third World countries, is all too familiar. Some Anglo-Saxon tribes, for example, had altered their basic pattern of life by the third century to accommodate the needs of the Roman traders. The daily pattern of agriculture had clearly changed as the Roman luxury trade ousted a traditional economy.

The pollen record suggests that a wide swathe of marginal land was cleared and brought into cultivation in early Roman times. Cereals, as well as a range of other crops, were being cultivated in places hitherto left overgrown. Village dwellings show similar changes as the economy expanded, and the population grew with it. Early Roman dwellings were like cottages, but these were soon rebuilt and in fact lengthened to accommodate livestock at one end. Cattle, it seems, had become an increasingly important asset. But, with time, the byres of the long house were modified to house craftsmen, and artisans – specialists making goods for local consumption as well as export – became a feature of village life. This all halted with the Roman recession, and in villages such as Vorbasse in Denmark and Feddersen Wierde in West Germany the agrarian regime appears to have fallen into recession as well. The pollen record shows that the area under cultivation receded, and while villages placed greater emphasis on their property rights, to judge from the new fences around their dwellings, some long houses were falling into disrepair.[4]

When the commerce between Rome and the barbarians began to flounder, the response of the stricken tribesmen was to raid for what they had earlier gained through trade. The two processes were not so different. Raiders evidently descended on vulnerable coastal settlements, and on merchant shipping. The Roman governor of Britain, Carausius, was alleged to have been in league with some of the pirates, and to have met them at sea where the booty was divided between the conspirators. Clearly the threat was sufficiently dangerous for the Romans to respond vigorously. Buffer communities or *foederati* – displaced migrants, attracted to the empire rather like present-day guest workers – were deliberately settled in vulnerable regions such as the Rhine mouth and south-east Britain and a string of forts and intermediary shore beacons were constructed along the coastlines of France, Flanders and Britain.

At the same time as these disturbances were unsettling Roman politicians, the climate in north-west Europe began to deteriorate. This deterioration exacerbated the already stressful circumstances in peripheral parts of north Germany and Jutland. A change of two to three degrees centigrade meant colder winters and shorter, wetter summers. It meant that the spring grass started growing later, and that much more hay had to be found for livestock during the longer winters. It meant that harvests in upland zones frequently failed; coastal zones experienced regular inundations from the North Sea, and river valleys frequently flooded. As a result, the agricultural cycle was put under severe stress. The same number of people had to be supported by fewer resources.[5] All of this inevitably led to social unrest which threatened the authority of the Germanic kings. In particular, the contests for declining resources would have squeezed some noble families as well as many peasants. In these circumstances it was time for the political refugees and the oppressed to seek opportunities elsewhere.

The crossing to Britain must have been an exhausting yet momentous experience. Like the arduous crossings to the United States it created legends and leaders. The few boats that have survived from this time, such as the Nydam ship, a large fourth century vessel found in a bog near Schleswig, north Germany, give us some impression of the challenge.[6] These were rowing boats equipped with only a small sail. Twenty to thirty people would have been at the oars with one or two men of greater strength taking charge of the steering oar at the back. There would have been only limited space in the

18. The Nydam ship

19. Carved ship prow

centre of the boat for luggage, and we must envisage the migrants coming with only the bare essentials of life. Some boats had savage-looking prows to intimidate and confuse the communities they passed along the way. We can imagine the passage in summertime: travelling from dawn to dusk at a steady eight to ten knots, great distances might be covered. At this speed the journey from Hamburg to Ostend might have taken four or five days. From Flanders to Kent, the Thames or East Anglia was a further day's journeying.

For these political refugees and their kinsfolk the crossing to Britain must have been an unforgettable adventure, recalled in stories that were handed down the generations. The crossing must have been perilous, especially for farmers who had scarcely travelled, yet unlike the journeys to the Americas it was soon completed. Moreover, the migrants beached in a landscape not so different from the one that they had left. Rolling hills with a coastal fringe of fens and marshes are common to west Jutland and eastern Britain. The social environment, too, was not so far removed from the one that they had known in the homelands. Following the withdrawal of the Roman administration Britain reverted to a system of tribal politics controlled, like the Anglo-Saxons, by elected leaders from established lineages. The world of towns and villas had dissolved; the landscape of eastern Britain was notable at that time for its decaying ruins within which many native leaders kept camp. Here too was a chiefdom society.

So the process was not so much an invasion as a migration. Over several decades, in groups of about thirty, Angles, Saxons and Jutes crossed to Kent, the Thames Valley, East Anglia and the Trent valley.[7] As many as several tens of thousands may have made the journey, although far fewer were involved in the invasion of Wessex recorded in the *Anglo-Saxon Chronicle*, and hardly more than a warband followed King Ida to Bernicia (northern Northumbria) to judge from the few cemeteries found in this region. When speculating upon the number of migrants we have to bear in mind that there were as many as a million natives in early fourth century Britain. By contrast, the migrants represented a small numerical threat, so we should not envisage them as invaders like the twenty to thirty thousand legionaries led by Vespasian in AD43 or the ten thousand Normans and Bretons led by Duke William in 1066. The migrations spanned almost two centuries, and the transformation from a Roman political system to an Anglo-Saxon one took many generations.

In some places, of course, the migrants did meet fierce resistance, and it was to be many decades before the Anglo-Saxon lineages gained supremacy. In other areas British leaders evidently employed Anglo-Saxon tribesmen as a buffer against further migrations.[8] But in most areas the transition was less dramatic and thus not remembered by later historians. Presumably the two communities integrated without rancour, and only after many generations did the German lineages assert their authority.

Most changes took place slowly, as if by stealth. For example, there is archaeological evidence that Anglo-Saxon settlers were in early fifth century Winchester long before the famous West Saxon invasion at the end of the century.[9] Saxon cemeteries with datable objects also occur in Wiltshire at least a century before the area was supposedly conquered. The course of this peaceful integration is well illustrated by the archaeology of Sussex. We can detect the initial coastal settlement in the fifth century, then the move inland indicated by later cemeteries, Anglo-Saxon settlements and place-names, and finally the settlement of the Sussex downlands and inland valleys by the seventh century.

The success of the Anglo-Saxons owed much to this peaceful integration. The farmers had taken a gamble leaving their homelands and, like any farmers, they must have been keen to settle down. By the

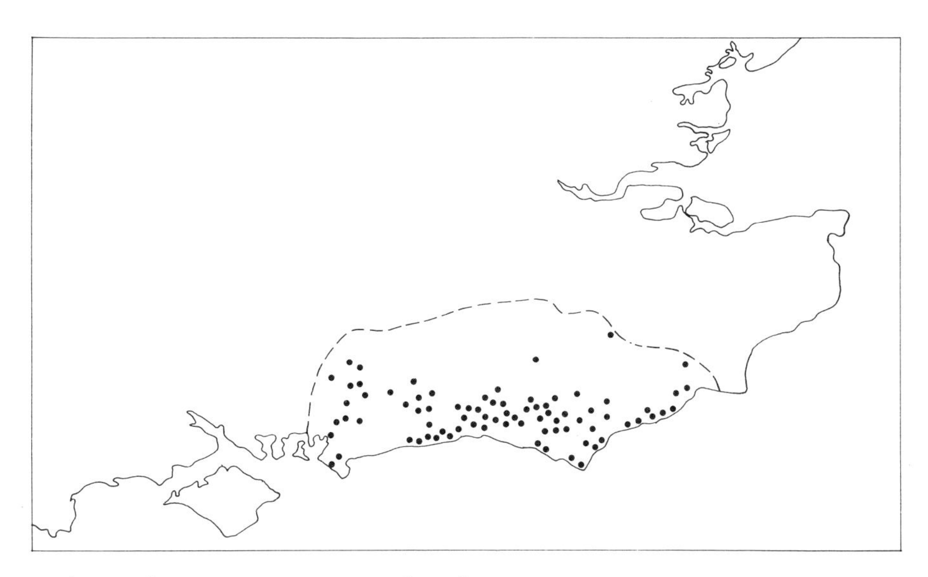

20. Anglo-Saxon settlement in Sussex

early sixth century (excavated) villages such as West Stow (Suffolk), recently reconstructed, were very much the norm.[10] Yet as the farmers adapted to the southern British environment, the descendants of prominent refugee families began to extend their authority, and the legacy of Rome became a dimmer memory. The first warrior leaders are apparent in the archaeological record from the early to mid-sixth century. In addition, place-names dating from this time confirm the class divisions within the migrant community.

Fifth century graves tend to contain only a few objects with the dead, betraying only limited differences in social standing. But by the middle of the sixth century the range and quality of the grave

21. The reconstructed Anglo-Saxon village at West Stow, Suffolk

accoutrements is quite remarkable. Recent analyses of these cemeteries point to at least four tiers within Anglo-Saxon society, and there may have been more.[11] The uppermost tiers seem to have been buried with pattern-welded swords (if they were men) or fine imported jewellery (if they were women); the next tier seems to be distinguished by the presence of lesser arms such as spears and seaxs (short, single-edged swords). The lowest ranks in sixth century society were buried with simple mementos: a knife, a buckle or a pin, while some were simply accorded a string of beads. Students of early English place-names have drawn attention to much the same thing. Sixth and seventh century names regularly consist of a compound of a man's name and the suffix *ingas* and *ingaham*, meaning homestead. Hence Reading was the homestead of Reada, and Wokingham the homestead of Wocca, each being the founder of the settlement.[12] And from these ranked societies emerged the kings whom Bede introduces us to in vivid terms as he chronicles the history of the English Church. Bede describes these first kings as warriors and it is as warriors that they evidently hoped to be remembered. Rich graves containing swords, shields and long knives are typical of the image. Perhaps the most spectacular example is the Sutton Hoo ship burial (see pages 54-6).

After a century of conflict between the principal lineages, the Anglo-Saxon aristocracy had assured itself of power when it espoused the new ideology, Christianity, and the Frankish wealth that came through trade connections with Christian countries. The long drawn out struggle for supremacy in England had meant that traditional Germanic codes were being modified, even abandoned. Anglo-Saxon dynasties, such as the Wuffingas of East Anglia, were not only able to ensure the succession of their sons to the leadership of the kingdom, but were also capable of raising sufficient rents and tribute to isolate the regal community as an elite from the rest of society. Leaders were no longer elected, and the rights of the aristocracy, as well as of the community as a whole, were suddenly altered. The king and the church were now making the rules.

One enigma remains unanswered, however. Many Britons had become Christians by the time the Romans left. How, therefore, did the pagan migrants mix with practitioners of this much newer religion? The answer eludes us at the moment. We do not know to what extent Christianity was espoused before AD400, and we are as ill-informed about Germanic ritual of this era.[13] It is assumed, however, that the leaders of Anglo-Saxon society also performed priestly duties, but this may not have always been the case. Only one temple has been excavated by archaeologists, and this was discovered close to the royal palace at Yeavering in Northumberland.[14] Whether the immigrants converted the native Britons, or whether Christianity

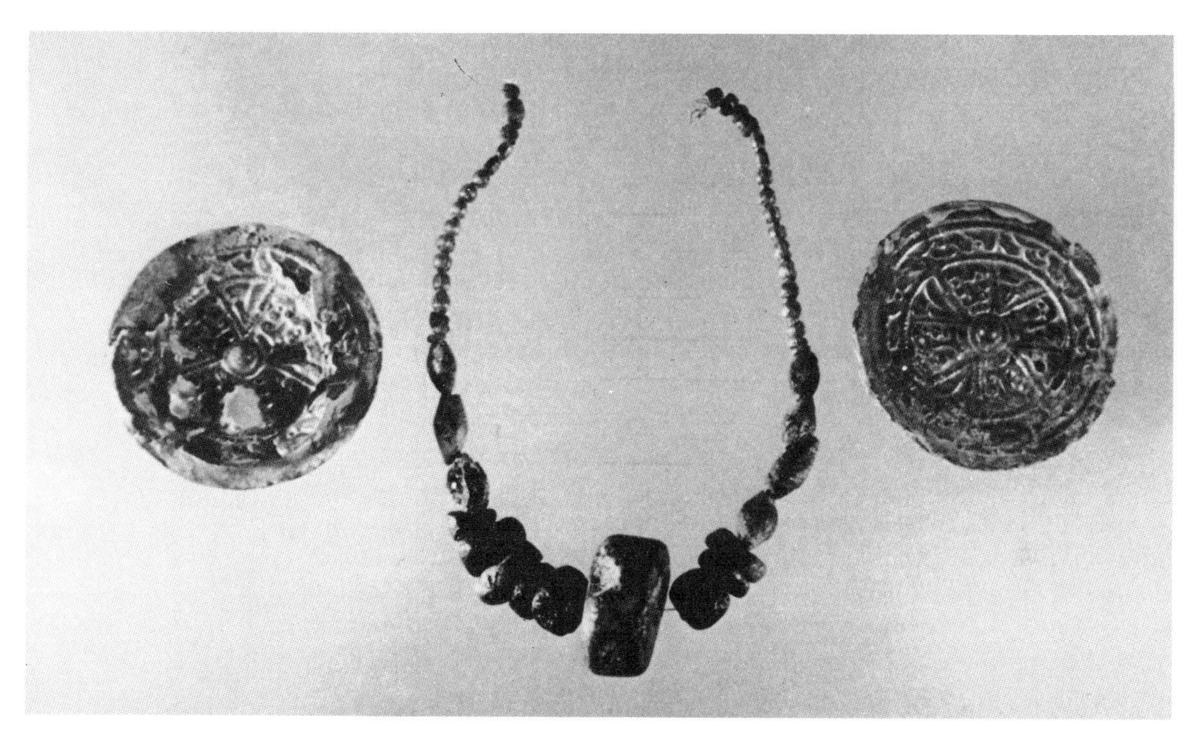

22. Anglo-Saxon grave goods from Winterbourne Gunner

was the religion of the Roman elite but not of the masses are intriguing questions for future research.

An enigma which we are less likely to resolve is much more fundamental to the history of the period. Why did the Picts and Scots who lived so much closer to Roman Britain not attempt to conquer the island when the legions left? Celtic kings, after all, had endured similar social problems to those we have identified in North Germany.

When the Roman economy began to decline, it put some pressure upon the Celtic kings who, like the Germans, had built up their power on a small quantity of imported prestige goods from the empire. Like the Anglo-Saxons, some Celtic chiefs instigated raids to acquire what previously had come by trade. Villas, towns and forts in western Britain suffered these sea-borne attacks, and of course, slaves such as St Patrick were taken in captivity to Ireland. The deterioration of the climate would have affected western Ireland, making it much wetter. So why was there no Irish migration comparable to the German one?

The answer, of course, is that there was. Celtic peoples began to migrate as social stress overwhelmed their communities.[15] Later historians recalled the Scots sailing from northern Ireland to south-west Scotland, Cornwall and Brittany – to environments which were close to their own. Britons from the south-west departed for France, establishing their own territory in north-west Gaul: Brittany. These communities stuck to the Irish coastal provinces where the landscape and possibly the language was familiar to them.

That no great leaders emerged from their ranks may, in part, result from the histories of their migrations. Bede, after all, has elevated Anglo-Saxon chiefs to arguably dizzy heights. Without his history how might we regard these first kings? Even so, the story of Celtic kingship over the following centuries is a striking contrast to the Anglo-Saxon experience.[16] Founded in the fifth century, the Celtic Church attained international status over the next two centuries, accumulating wealth and political power, and leaving kings and their courts to muse over Finn McCool and legendary leaders of the pre-Christian period. As far as we can tell, the church prohibited marriage within lineages – a traditional means by which lineages protected their accumulated wealth – and encouraged marriage alliances between lineages. This weakened the lineages, and the women who were married for alliance purposes looked to the church for support in such circumstances. Thus the church acquired property, as well as power. Although the Celtic Church appears to have impeded the development of warrior kings, the evidence for the plight of kingship is slight. If Christianity had been introduced two centuries later, one wonders whether the course of these migrations, as well as Irish and Scottish history, might have resembled the experience of Anglo-Saxon England.

The seeds of the migrations lay back in the era of Augustus when his legions and merchants probed the interior and coasts of Germania. The decision to abandon the coastlines of north Germany and Jutland in the fifth century was a response to a number of problems. The decline of the empire greatly affected the status of local chiefs who had come to depend on imported luxuries to sustain their prowess within the community. Being coastal communities these peoples had to bear the brunt of the deterioration of the climate. High spring tides in particular, and uncertain conditions for harvests on marginal lands must have compelled them to take the drastic decision to uproot themselves. Political refugees, squeezed by these circumstances, may have taken the initiative, but the archaeology does not lead us to regard these migrations as invasions. Some warriors evidently took part, but most were farmers in search of new opportunities, hoping to slip into niches left vacant as the Roman government in Britain unceremoniously departed.

We must imagine small-scale invasions, landings around the coastline, in the early fifth century, followed by a period of integration lasting at least two generations. Around AD500, the era of the legendary Arthur, some sub-Roman chiefs and the aspiring German lineages fought for status and territory. It is often couched in civilised Roman terms, but was clearly akin to the squabbles between warbands in pre-Roman times. These warriors were the grandfathers of the first kings. Grandfathers and grandsons, of course, are remembered by historians if they were involved in dispute, but the prevalent oral tradition of the time, telling of the peaceful integration of two ethnically different communities, was not written down by later monks. Archaeology alone balances the picture of warrior graves – how sixth century leaders wished to be seen – with the farmhouses and peaceful existence of their daily lives. It was, ironically, the status offered by a new ideology – Christianity – and all the manufactured kitchenware and bangles that it brought, as well as the access to a wider world, that caused these warriors to forsake their immediate heritage.

As the history of Britain comes more clearly into view with the adoption of Christianity, we have a picture of an island divided into two.[17] The western and northern half was in the hands of countless Celtic leaders, while the southern and eastern half was controlled by a new German aristocracy.

## Further reading

L. Alcock, *Arthur's Britain* (London, 1971); M. Gelling, *Signposts to the Past: Place-names and the History of England* (London, 1981); J. Goody, *The Domestication of the Savage Mind* (Cambridge, 1977); C. Thomas, *Christianity in Roman Britain to AD500* (London, 1981); D.M. Wilson, *The Northern World: the History and Heritage of Northern Europe, AD400-1100* (London, 1980).

CHAPTER FOUR

# The Emergence of Anglo-Saxon Kingdoms

Patrick Wormald

In AD597 a large and high-powered body of Christian missionaries arrived in the pagan kingdom of Kent. They had been sent from Rome by Pope Gregory 'the Great' (590-604), in the hope of bringing people that Gregory called the 'Angles' (or English) from heathen darkness into Christian light. Whatever else they achieved, they certainly brought new light into Anglo-Saxon history, because Christianity meant literacy and literacy means written historical sources. Thanks to these sources, above all to the great *Ecclesiastical History of the English People*[1] by the Venerable Bede, which was completed in 731, we know far more about the seventh and eighth centuries than about earlier times. Nevertheless, to the modern eye, the political map of early Christian England looks remote and unfamiliar. Even the four great kingdoms, whose emergence is the most striking historical feature of the two centuries after 597, survive today largely as police authorities or water boards.

We do not really know how many kingdoms there were in Germanic Britain at the start of this period. Historians used to speak of a 'heptarchy', or 'seven kingdoms', but there were at least a dozen, quite probably many more. According to Bede, there were kingdoms of the Jutes in Kent itself and the Isle of Wight; there were kingdoms of the East, South and West Saxons (respectively Essex, Sussex and Wessex); there were kingdoms of the Angles in East Anglia, Mercia, Deira and Bernicia, and also an obscure and apparently amorphous group of Middle Angles in the East Midlands. The map shows others, such as the kingdom of Lindsey (Lincolnshire) and that of the Hwicce

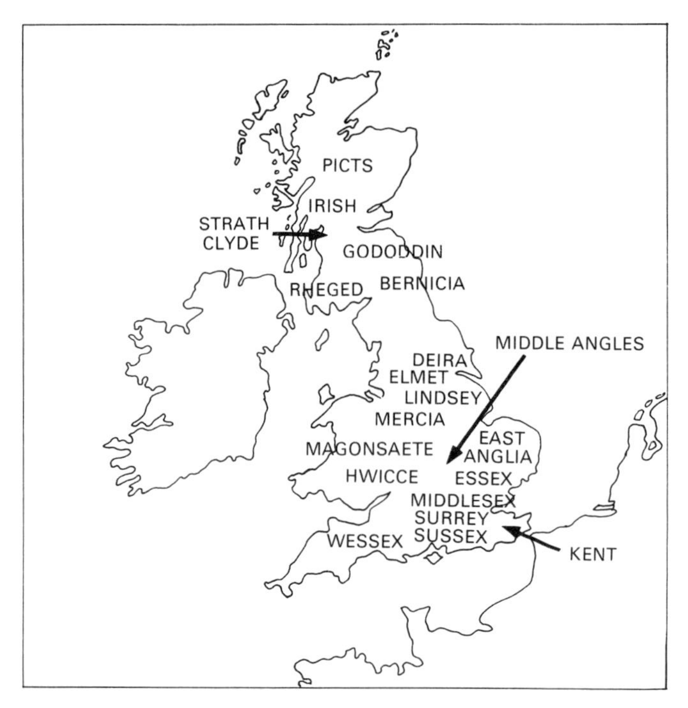

23. The kingdoms of Britain c.597

(Gloucestershire and Worcestershire); and, to judge from its name, there may have been another in Middlesex with its *south region* in *Sur-rey*.[2] It should be noted that even this plethora of political fragments covered a much smaller area than present-day England; the four south-western counties, plus Hereford, Shropshire, Cheshire, Lancashire and Cumbria, were still in the hands of the Britons, or, as the Anglo-Saxons called them, the Welsh.

Two hundred years later, when the Viking raids began to usher in a new era, there were, in effect, only four kingdoms left, but these were considerably more powerful than any of their early seventh century predecessors. The area settled and often ruled by Anglo-Saxons had expanded to the modern English borders and, in the north, beyond. Within this area, the greater kingdoms had swallowed the smaller ones. The four surviving kingdoms were: Northumbria, uniting Deira and Bernicia and extending from the Humber and the Ribble to the Forth and the Southern Uplands; Mercia, incorporating all the kingdoms between Wales and the Fens, the Humber and the Thames, and also, for a time, the south and east of England; East Anglia, by now much the least significant, and dominated by Mercia for a generation before 825, but thereafter independent until the Vikings struck in 869; and finally Wessex which, having absorbed the Isle of Wight and British territory as far west as the Tamar, seized control of the south-east from Mercia after 825, and was eventually to form the

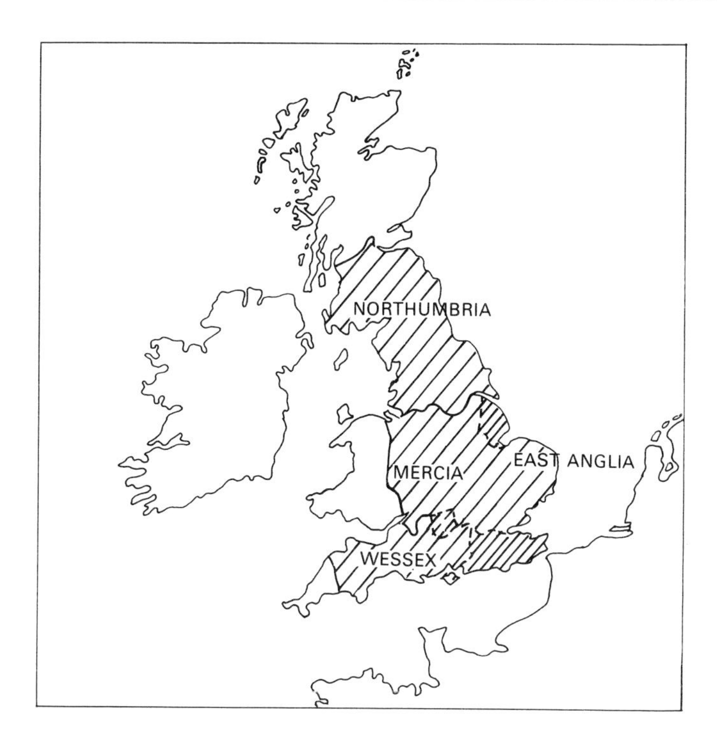


24. The Anglo-Saxon kingdoms c.825

united kingdom of the English. What concerns us here is the way these few great kingdoms emerged out of the much more variegated political landscape, *c*.597. Why was it that these kingdoms established their power? How did they govern and exploit their territory? What explains the fluctuations of power that made Kent, Surrey and Sussex first Mercian, then West Saxon, and made East Anglia, Northumbria, Mercia and Wessex each in turn 'top kingdom'? Finally, is it possible to see in all this a drift towards the eventual unification of England?

We may begin with a more detailed look at the history of one of these kingdoms, Mercia, for most of this period the most powerful.[3] Mercia originated, perhaps no earlier than the mid-sixth century, as the kingdom of the 'March' (i.e. border with the Britons) along the upper waters of the Trent. Early medieval kings did not have what we would call capitals, but it was at Tamworth that Mercian kings liked to spend Christmas, which is not a bad index of where they felt most at home, and the original Mercian bishopric, doubtless sited for easy access to the king, was at Lichfield. Mercia's first great king was Penda. He began a spectacular career by overrunning the Hwicce, *c*.628, and killing the Northumbrian king in battle five years later. He went on to dispose similarly of one other king of Northumbria and no less than three kings of East Anglia, whilst also driving the king of Wessex from his throne for three years. He extended Mercian authority over the Middle Angles, and established a principality in

25. (left) Offa's gold dinar
26. (right) Offa's silver penny

Herefordshire. Finally, in 655, he again attacked Northumbria with a vast army containing, according to Bede, 'thirty royal leaders' and their 'legions'; but this time he was defeated and killed.[4]

The abrupt end of Penda's splendid record did not terminate Mercian power. Under his son, Wulfhere (658-74), and later under Aethelbald (716-57), Mercia consolidated its grip on central England, including London, and continued to threaten the areas beyond. The greatest king of this period, Offa (757-96), was by the end of his reign the king of all of England south of the Humber, apart from Wessex. He persistently attacked the Welsh, and built his great dyke along almost the whole length of the Welsh frontier (twice as long as Hadrian's Wall). He was the first Anglo-Saxon king to issue coins in his own name on a large scale. From his correspondence, it emerges that the great Frankish emperor Charlemagne (768-814), the most powerful ruler in Europe between the Romans and Napoleon, was prepared to treat him as an equal. But the structure of even Offa's power was unsound. In eighth century Anglo-Saxon politics, a king was rarely succeeded by his son or brother, and very distant relatives often seized the throne; Offa himself succeeded a remote cousin after fighting a civil war. We are told in a contemporary letter that he 'shed much blood' in disposing of rivals to his son's succession,[5] but his son survived him by a mere six months, and *his* successor, Cenwulf (796-821), was Offa's fourth cousin twice removed! Moreover, Offa's death signalled instant rebellion against Mercian rule in Kent and East Anglia. Cenwulf restored Mercian control, but he was the last great

Mercian king. Between 821 and 827 there were four kings of Mercia, each, it seems, from a different royal line; East Anglia recovered its independence; and King Egbert of Wessex (802-39), Alfred's grandfather, overran the south-east. Not even the most powerful kings were able to establish a permanent ascendancy for their dynasty or kingdom.

We can put flesh and blood on the dry bones of these events by considering the vernacular literature of the Anglo-Saxons, above all the long epic poem, *Beowulf*.[6] This survives only in a manuscript of *c.*1000, and it concerns the heroes of pagan Scandinavia, *c.*500, but it is an English poem and, although its date of composition is controversial, there are hints of a connection with Mercia during or shortly after the reign of Offa.

It could be that *Beowulf* reflects the conditions and conventions of Anglo-Saxon society, just as Dickens reflects those of Victorian England. The poem is about kings and their aristocratic warriors. When not engaged in battle with human foes, or monsters such as the troll, Grendel, and the Dragon, kings reside in great halls, where they dispense hospitality (especially of the liquid variety) to their personal retainers, and make gifts to them of gold rings, weapons and lands. (Readers of the romances of J.R.R. Tolkien will find much here that they recognise, for the excellent reason that Tolkien was a noted expert on the poem.)

In return for a king's generosity, his followers owe him loyalty to the point of death. At the end of the poem, when Beowulf lies mortally wounded by the Dragon, his one faithful follower excoriates the others who had fled in terror:

> Anyone who cares to speak the truth can say that the king who gave you the valuable arms which you now bear . . . utterly squandered them. . . . Now the receiving of treasure, the giving of swords, and every enjoyment of home and happiness must cease for you and your families. . . . To any fighting man death is better than a life of dishonour.[7]

An important feature of this relationship is that a king's following included many foreigners, adventurers or exiles from other kingdoms, who were lured to his hall and banner by the prospect of victory and the loot that was victory's reward. Beowulf entered the service of Hrothgar, king of the Danes, though he was himself a prince from Gotland in southern Sweden. 'Such success in arms and so great a fame attended Hrothgar', says the poet, 'that . . . the number of his young retainers increased until he had a formidable army.'[8] The greatest kings in the world of the poem were those who could attract

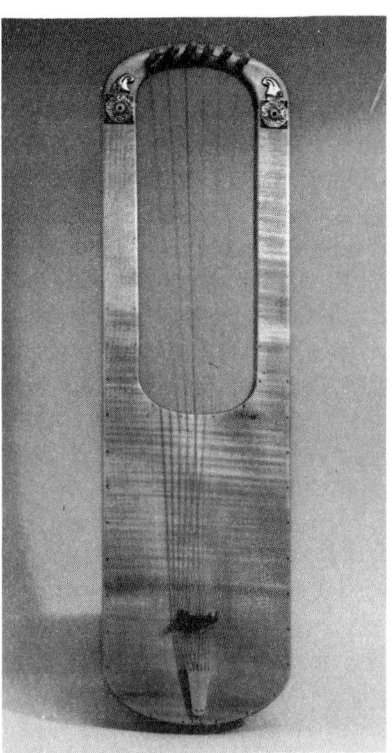

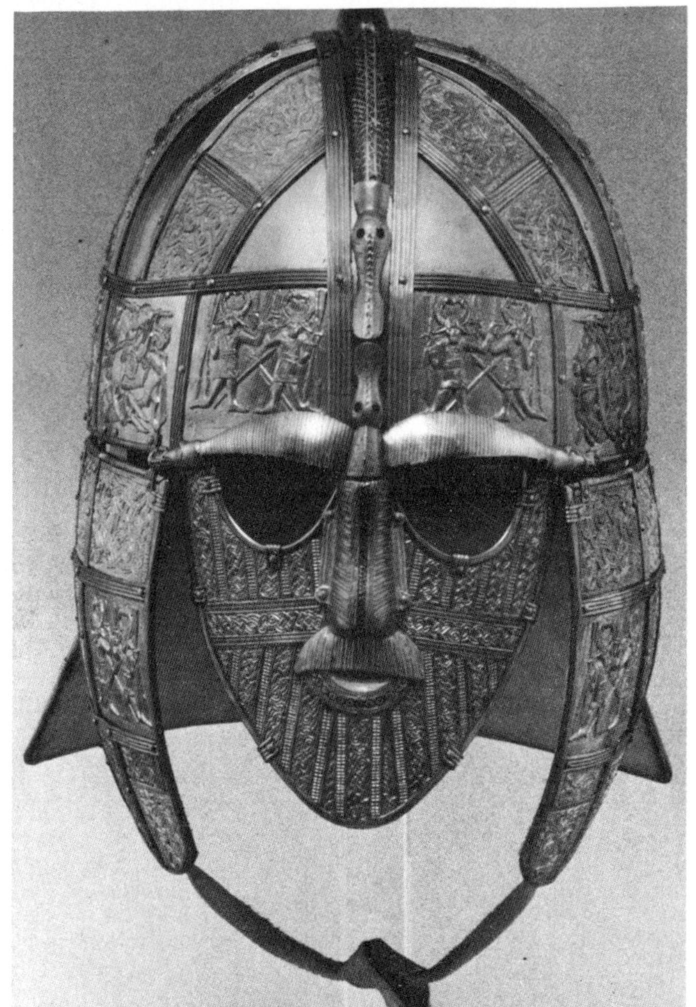

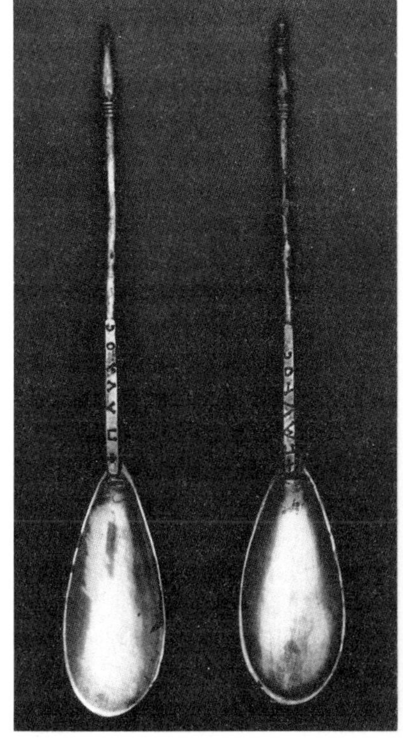

27, 28, 29. Treasures from the Sutton Hoo ship burial

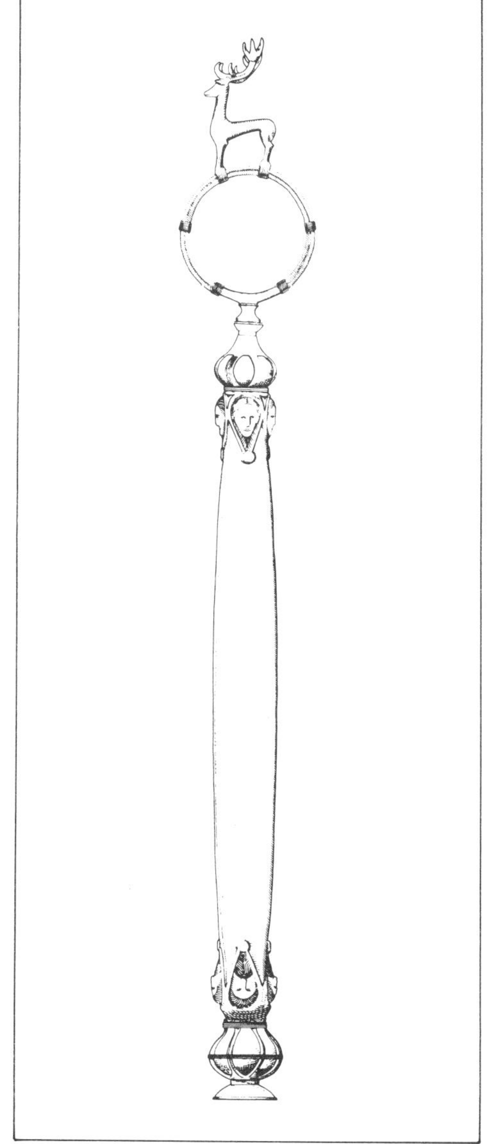

the best warriors, and they did so by seeming the most likely to be able to offer plunder, lands and glory.

Historical sources from seventh and eighth century England do tell of such mobile bands of aristocratic warriors, transferring their services to the most generous kings or fighting and plundering on their own account. But the resemblances between the world of *Beowulf* and that of England in our period are underlined above all by one of the most sensational archaeological discoveries of the twentieth century, the great ship-burial at Sutton Hoo in Suffolk.[9] Here an early seventh century potentate, presumably a king of East Anglia, had been interred in a substantial ship, surrounded by a spectacular collection of weapons and treasures. The weapons included a helmet, a mail-coat, a sword and a shield, spears and axes. Among the treasures were superb shoulder-clasps in gold and garnet *cloisonné*, bowls both of Celtic and Egyptian origin, a large silver dish from the eastern Mediterranean and a purse of gold coins from Frankish Gaul; there was also a harp and some drinking-horns. Now there are various close links between this burial and *Beowulf*. Several of the objects have affinities with Scandinavia, where the poem is set, including the helmet, which looks exactly like one described by the poet. The poem begins with Scyld, founder of the Danish royal house, being laid in his ship amongst his treasures and cast out to sea, and it ends with the entombment of Beowulf himself in a barrow on a cliff-top; a conflation of the two would give one something very like Sutton Hoo. Indeed, the only known ship-burials elsewhere in the Europe of this period were in central Sweden. But what is more important is that poem and burial share a common atmosphere. Commemorated at Sutton Hoo was a king with things to give: loot and weapons such as might well attract warriors to his service, and drink and music with which to entertain them. It seems, then, that something similar to the poem's world of kings did exist in seventh century England.

If this is so, we have to ask a more prosaic question than would ever have concerned the poet: how was the high life of kings and noblemen supported? They needed more food, mineral resources and building materials than plunder would provide; and they needed a system which would supply them. It is of course true that early Anglo-Saxon society and government were by modern standards primitive. But we know from anthropologists working on 'primitive' societies today that even wholly illiterate governments, depending on memory and word of mouth, can achieve impressive feats of organisation. In any case, Anglo-Saxon kings from the seventh century onwards did issue codes of law, like that of Aethelbert of Kent (d.616), the first English Christian king, and also charters, written titles to property and privilege in favour of churches and eventually of lay followers. These sources reveal that retainers pledged to a king in love and loyalty could serve as his officers in central and local government. They also show the sort of resources he could command.

The most important of these resources were his lands, because these supplied food-rents to support himself and his household followers. The basis on which this was worked out was the most fundamental unit of Anglo-Saxon society and government, the hide. Bede defined a hide as the amount of land that would support a single freeman and his family.[10] It should be noted that this is a unit of yield, not of size: it measures the produce of land whose actual acreage would have varied with its fertility. And because the hidage, or assessment in hides, of a piece of land revealed what it could produce, it also told a lord how much food he could collect from it himself, much as parsons used to take tithes. What this could mean in practical terms is shown by the amount of food-rent owed by ten hides (about ten families) to the King of Wessex every year, according to a law of the late seventh century: '10 vats of honey, 300 loaves, 12 measures of Welsh ale, 30 of clear ale, 2 full-grown cows or 10 wethers, 10 geese, 20 hens, 10 cheeses, a measure of butter, 5 salmon, 20 pounds of fodder and 100 eels.'[11]

Now it is obvious that taxation of this kind posed problems of collection and storage exceeding even those of the EEC's agricultural policy. This brings us to a second key unit of the system, the royal vill

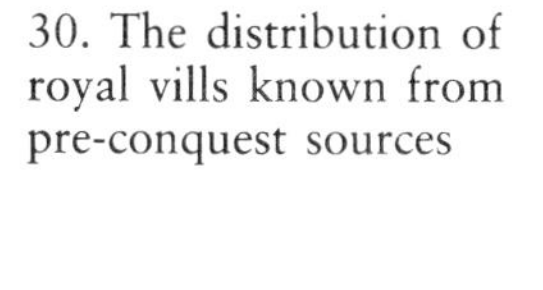
30. The distribution of royal vills known from pre-conquest sources

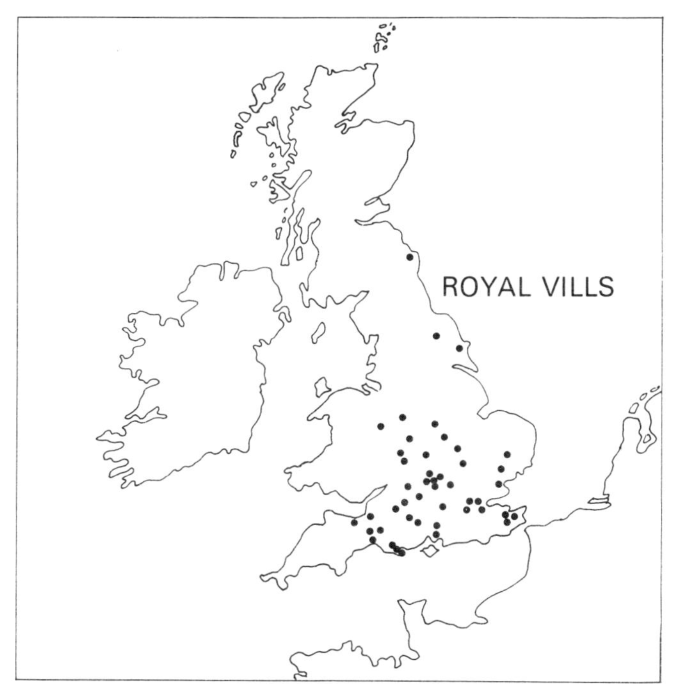

or manor. Kings, as we have seen, did not have capitals in the modern sense; they had a large number of different royal estates scattered around their kingdoms. These were probably the bases of the king's local government officers, ealdormen or reeves. It was here that, in many parts of England, the local lawcourt met and the king's officer collected his fines. It was also at these manors that the king's local food-rents would be deposited; the point was that kings moved continuously around their domains, from one royal vill to the next, consuming what had been left at each. In other words, the taxation system was geared to supplying the king and his court with a hot meal on their travels. Royal halls such as those in *Beowulf* were not only scenes of upper-class jollification but also centres which exploited a king's agricultural resources. And in areas where the king controlled salt, iron or lead mines, they would have been used to collect and distribute these less perishable commodities too.[12]

Quite apart from what was due to the king from his own property, it appears that he had rights over all his subjects. He could demand hospitality for himself, his agents, even his hounds and horses, at manors that were not his own. He could also demand military service, and work on bridges, fortifications and royal palaces from all freemen. And because the hidage of a piece of land revealed not only what it could produce but also the number of heads of household it theoretically supported, hides could be used to assess the number of men obliged to work for the king, whether in war or peace. Offa's Dyke was presumably the fruit of such obligations and is spectacular testimony to their efficacy. One of the most intriguing (and tantalisingly obscure) documents to survive from this period is known as the *Tribal Hidage*. It assigns round numbers of hides to every kingdom except Northumbria, beginning with the Mercians: it could just be the assessment for hospitality and military or labour service of his whole vast dominion by one of the great Mercian kings. If so, it is evidence of a far more sophisticated administrative system than we can easily imagine.[13]

There is good reason to think that this system was changing and developing during this period. Kings needed even more than their own estates and mines could produce: wine, for example, or the sort of lava that made the best whetstones for honing swords. Such commodities were supplied by trade with other countries. Whatever kings had plenty of (for example, slaves captured on campaign) was exchanged for what they wanted. Increasingly, kings derived a direct income from this trade. For one thing, they took tolls on it: a charter of Aethelbald, dated 733, grants the church at Rochester remission of the customs payable at London.[14] Even more important, kings of the second half of the eighth century were the first rulers in Britain since the Romans to mint coins in their own name.[15] The growth of trade had prompted the minting of money in England since the mid-seventh century, first in gold, then in silver. The distribution of early eighth century coin-finds suggests that they were used not only in overseas trade but also in local markets.[16] But until the 750s English coins did not bear a king's name, and may well have been issued by prosperous traders, like the original banknotes. Thereafter, we do have a royal coinage, indeed almost nothing but a royal coinage; and the coinage of Offa was as widely distributed as previous anonymous issues. Money-making (in the literal sense) was a lucrative business, so long as coins still consisted of precious metal. It is likely enough that Offa's coinage was a new and highly profitable royal monopoly, and that a more monetarised economy fed royal wealth.

This sort of administrative system could make some kings very powerful. But we have seen that, although the political history of seventh and eighth century England was one of pike swallowing minnows, no one ever quite managed to become the only fish in the pond. To understand this, we may return to *Beowulf*. In the poem, the most effective kings were those who attracted the best warriors by offering the best opportunities. In the world of the poem's probable audience, the kingdoms that flourished were those to the north and west, those with an open frontier against the Celts; the reason must be that they had most to offer in loot and lands. Thus, a king such as Penda could come to dominate his Welsh and English neighbours because, as Bede's account of his final battle suggests, he could attract the largest number of noble and well-equipped warriors. The successors of the wealthy East Anglian king buried at Sutton Hoo had less to offer, quite simply because Penda was in the way: he killed three of them.

Yet the fate of the once-mighty East Anglian kingdom, and ultimately of Mercia itself, is a warning that power like this had built-in obsolescence. The *Beowulf* poet is vividly aware that nemesis awaits the greatest kings, and he shows why. The essence of successful kingship is generosity. It is significant that the only way we know about the resources and rights of early Anglo-Saxon kings, in an age that had no government documents as such, is because we have the charters in which these resources and rights were granted away. Constant generosity means that more loot must constantly be garnered, new raids perpetually launched. With all the luck in the world, this is eventually impossible, biologically or geographically or both; and when the limit is reached, warriors will seek fresh pastures. Royal power is like a snowball: while it moves it grows, but when it stops it melts. Moreover, such fundamentally predatory kingship accumulates as many enemies as treasures. Kings had potential enemies in their own families, envious of their power and wealth, and real enemies in those kinsmen whose ambitions they had forestalled by banishment, and in those rival dynasties they had decimated or humbled. Both in *Beowulf* and in seventh and eighth century England, we find a throng of exiles, awaiting the opportunity of revenge. Beowulf himself, foreseeing the outbreak of renewed hostility between the Danes and their neighbours at the very wedding-feast designed to bring peace, observes sardonically: 'After the death of a prince, it seldom happens that the spear lies idle for long, however beautiful the bride may be.'[17] So kingdoms are rather like public companies: they depend on warrior shareholders, and adverse profits of war prompt a panic which then permits a takeover by internal or external rivals. Hence, the pattern of fluctuating competition in political circles, the upper levels of society, for resources that were so well-organised below that a change of owner was relatively easy.

Finally, and in the light of all this, is it possible to say that the eventual unification of the English kingdoms was inherent in the logic of seventh and eighth century politics? Bede describes how seven Anglo-Saxon kings from various kingdoms, between the late fifth and the late seventh centuries, were overlords of all the southern English kingdoms, and he describes their power as an *imperium* – an empire. In the late ninth century, the *Anglo-Saxon Chronicle* gives these same kings, plus Egbert of Wessex, the vernacular title of *Bretwalda*, a word which appears to mean 'ruler of Britain'. And an important charter of Aethelbald of Mercia, dated 736, calls him 'King not only of the Mercians but of all the South English', and also 'King of Britain'.[18] We seem to have here an institution which pointed the way towards a union of at least the southern English peoples, and which it was somehow appropriate to call rule of Britain as a whole. Many historians have thought that the office had defined rights and prerogatives which ultimately transcended the often sordid realities of Anglo-Saxon internecine warfare.

But we have seen that, however stable and effective the administrative systems of early Christian England were, its political structure was surprisingly fragile.[19] Even Offa's power could hardly be sustained after his death, because power like his was resented, resisted and rebelled against. One highly significant feature of the lists of *Bretwaldas* in Bede and the *Anglo-Saxon Chronicle* is that they do not contain a single king of Mercia although, from Penda to Cenwulf, Mercian kings were on all other evidence the most powerful Anglo-Saxon rulers. The reason is probably that Bede was a Northumbrian and the *Anglo-Saxon Chronicle* was written in Wessex: each was unwilling to record the supremacy of rivals and enemies. Such sentiments were no basis for cosy political consensus among Anglo-

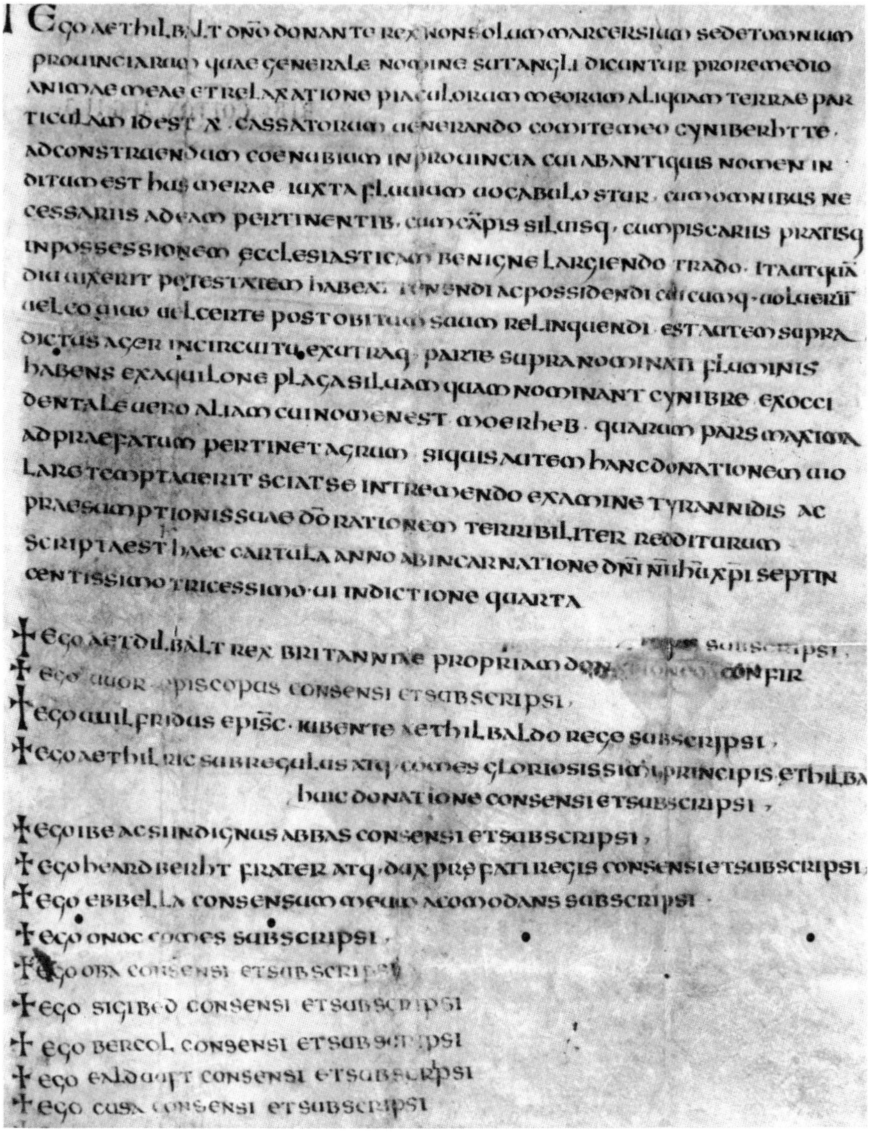
Ego Aethilbalt dno donante rex non solum Marcersium sed et omnium
provinciarum quae generale nomine Sutangli dicuntur pro remedio
animae meae et relaxatione piaculorum meorum aliquam terrae par
ticulam id est x cassatorum venerando comite meo Cyniberhtte
ad construendum coenubium in provincia cui ab antiquis nomen in
ditum est Husmerae iuxta fluvium vocabulo Stur cum omnibus ne
cessariis ad eam pertinentib. cum campis silvisq. cum piscariis pratisq
in possessionem ecclesiasticam benigne largiendo trado. Ita ut quam
diu vixerit potestatem habeat tenendi ac possidendi cuicumq. voluerit
vel eo vivo vel certe post obitum suum relinquendi. est autem supra
dictus ager in circuitu ex utraq. parte supranominati fluminis
habens ex aquilone plaga silvam quam nominant Cynibre ex occi
dentale vero aliam cui nomen est Moerheb. quarum pars maxima
ad praefatum pertinet agrum. siquis autem hanc donationem vio
lare temptaverit sciat se in tremendo examine tyrannidis ac
praesumptionis suae Dō rationem terribiliter redditurum
Scripta est haec cartula anno ab incarnatione dni nri ihu xpi septin
centissimo tricessimo vi indictione quarta
+ Ego Aetdilbalt rex Britanniae propria manu ... subscripsi ... confir
+ Ego Uuor episcopus consensi et subscripsi
+ Ego Uuilfridus episc. iubente Aethilbaldo rege subscripsi
+ Ego Aethilric subregulus atq. comes gloriosissimi principis Ethilba
huic donatione consensi et subscripsi
+ Ego Ibe acsi indignus abbas consensi et subscripsi
+ Ego Heardberht frater atq. dux praefati regis consensi et subscripsi
+ Ego Ebbella consensum meum acomodans subscripsi
+ Ego Onoc comes subscripsi
+ Ego Oba consensi et subscripsi
+ Ego Sigibed consensi et subscripsi
+ Ego Bercol consensi et subscripsi
+ Ego Ealduuft consensi et subscripsi
+ Ego Cusa consensi et subscripsi

31. Charter of King Aethelbald 'Rex Britanniae'

Saxon kingdoms. Unlike the continental kingdoms, England did not begin as a single political unit in the more or less immediate aftermath of the barbarian invasions, yet the continental kingdoms tended to fragment and were ultimately unified centuries after England itself. This suggests that there can have been nothing automatic about English unification. No Anglo-Saxon kingdom was consistently powerful enough to overcome all the resentments that their ascendancy incurred – until the Vikings left only one kingdom standing in King Alfred's Wessex.

There is, however, a catch. We *can* say that, by Offa's day, some

Anglo-Saxons considered themselves as belonging, in some sense, to a single English people, a *gens Anglorum*. The title of Bede's history shows that he did, and he was not alone. Administratively unifiable (perhaps); politically fragmented (certainly); the Anglo-Saxons were already, culturally, becoming one people. I would suggest, tentatively, that the explanation lies in one of history's extraordinary accidents. Some time before he became pope, Gregory the Great met a group of Anglo-Saxon slaves in the market-place in Rome. They impressed him so much that he coined a notorious pun: 'not Angles but Angels'; and he determined that he would see to their conversion.[20] Romans such as Gregory had tidy minds and liked to think that each one-time Roman province was dominated by a single barbarian people, as Gaul was by the Franks. Now the Anglo-Saxons that Gregory met actually *were* Angles: they were from Deira. Gregory became convinced that all barbarians in Britain were Angles. At the time, it was normal to refer to Britain's invaders as Saxons (and the Scots still call Englishmen 'Sassenachs'). But Gregory invariably wrote of 'Angles', so he sent his missionaries to found the 'Church of the English', the *ecclesia Anglorum*. The church that they did found, at Canterbury, was committed from the outset to the view that it was responsible for a single English people, and its view gradually percolated through to its flock, via churchmen such as Bede himself. The first 'Englishmen' were perhaps more conscious of their common identity in the next world than in this. But that was one of the most important reasons why the Anglo-Saxons eventually outgrew their warrior adolescence and became the first European state to assume something like its present shape and structure.

## Further reading

Bede's *Ecclesiastical History*, trans. L. Sherley-Price (Harmondsworth, 1965); *Beowulf*, trans. M. Alexander (Harmondsworth, 1973) – verse; *Beowulf*, trans. D. Wright (London, 1973) – prose; R. Bruce-Mitford, *The Sutton Hoo Ship Burial, a handbook* (London, 1972); J. Campbell (ed.), *The Anglo-Saxons*, chs 2-5, (Oxford, 1982); D. Hill, *An Atlas of Anglo-Saxon England* (Oxford, 1981).

CHAPTER FIVE

# Picts, Scots and Britons

## Wendy Davies

Far more than half of Britain lay beyond the area of Anglo-Saxon settlement in the fifth and sixth centuries – a very large area, of considerable geographical and economic diversity. The sources of information about it are limited and difficult to use but, although we must always be aware of the limitations of this evidence, we do have some knowledge and we do know that these parts of Britain cannot be reduced to a uniform background of wild natives.[1] Popular views of these parts at that time are invariably conditioned by two predominant images: the image of heroic society on the one hand and of a proliferation of ascetic saints on the other. In fact both images are misleading and, if anything, hinder understanding about this area of Britain during the period of Saxon settlement and consolidation from the fifth to the eighth century.

Let us consider, first, the value of the popular images. The image of heroic society is dominated by warbands – men attracted from afar to the leadership of famous lords – drinking rapaciously in the halls of their leaders before going out to battle, receiving gifts and fighting faithfully in return.[2] This image of military lordship is powerfully and memorably expressed in the early Welsh stanzas known as *The Gododdin*, a long set of elegiac verses describing an unsuccessful expedition from the neighbourhood of Edinburgh to a place called Catraeth, probably Catterick. Like most of the genre, this is a poem of defeat:

> From the retinue of Mynyddog they hastened forth; in a shining array they fed together round the wine-vessel. My heart has become full of grief for the feast of Mynyddog, I have lost too many of my true kinsmen. Out of three hundred wearing gold torques who hastened to Catraeth, alas, none escaped but for one man. . . . He

> was a man reared and nourished on wine, of generous heart; he was a blessed, active man, he was a wearer of a broad mailcoat, he was fierce, he was rash, on the back of his horse.[3]

The other image, by contrast, is of physical passivity: of very holy men who retreated from society in search of spiritual purity. They opted for restraint and moderation, without material comfort, without social and family support, in solitude or with only a few companions – withdrawing, typically, to islands off the coast but sometimes journeying to unfamiliar parts, leaving a trail of memory and influence as they travelled. This image is repeatedly conveyed by the type of text known as 'Lives of Saints'; thus, in the late eleventh century the cleric Rhigyfarch wrote of St David:

> Such an austerity did the holy father decree in his zeal for the monastic system, that every monk toiled at daily labour, and spent his life working with his hands for the community. 'For who does not work', says the apostle, 'let him not eat.' Knowing that carefree rest was the source and the mother of vices he bowed down the shoulders of the monks with pious labours, for those who bow heads and minds in leisurely repose develop a spirit of instability and apathy with restless promptings to lust. . . . After matins, the holy father proceeded alone to hold converse with the angels. Immediately afterwards, he sought cold water, remaining in it sufficiently long to subdue all the ardours of the flesh. The whole day he spent, inflexibly and unweariedly, in teaching, praying, genuflecting, and in care for the brethren; also in feeding a multitude of orphans, wards, widows, needy, sick, feeble, and pilgrims.[4]

We are conditioned, therefore, to think of men fighting a desperate last ditch stand or fighting a spiritual battle and retreating into sanctity.

Neither of these images is very helpful, for two particular reasons. First, the written sources which express the images derive from later periods than the events described; they do not provide contemporary evidence. The poetry is at the least an amalgam of sixth to ninth century (or even later) material and cannot be used as evidence for anything earlier than the ninth century. The Saints' Lives, with a few exceptions, were written at varying dates from the ninth century onwards, with the greatest number in the late eleventh and twelfth centuries.[5] Both types of source are much more useful evidence of the values and attitudes of the societies which produced them than of the events of the fifth, sixth, seventh or eighth centuries.

The second reason is that the popular images conceal differences between societies and divert attention from the fragmentary, earlier source material that does exist. The island of Britain is an area of considerable geographical variety. Mountainous areas such as north Wales and highland Scotland do not support the same sorts of living as the rich farm lands in Fife or the Vale of Glamorgan, and whereas people in Fife and Glamorgan in the early Middle Ages depended essentially on farming, life in the western coastlands of Scotland looked seawards, while those living near the forests of south-west Wales drew on hunting as well as farming. Such differences in environment affected more than the outlook, for the rich farm lands of Glamorgan could support far more production than the poorer lands of Anglesey or Cornwall. Some environments, then, would have produced a surplus and others would have supported no more than basic subsistence. Where there was a surplus it was sometimes (but not always) sufficient to support a leisured aristocracy. Thus geographical differences might affect the type of social group that the land supported. Of course, they also often impeded communications. Mountains and forests – and fens like the Somerset levels – made contact between groups difficult, producing fragmentation and isolation and, therefore, differing development.

There was diversity too in background: even in the relatively recent past not all of Britain had been part of a Roman province and within the Roman provinces some regions had been far more influenced by Mediterranean technology and material culture than others. South-east Wales, for example, had had many Romanised country houses and estates while Cumbria and Cornwall had not. And there are other differences in background: south-west Scotland probably had a long tradition of contact with northern Ireland, and Devon and Cornwall may have had the same with Brittany. Cornwall at least had a long history of wide-ranging foreign contacts because of its tin mines.

There was also linguistic diversity. Two distinct sets of languages (both Celtic) were represented, Goidelic and Brittonic, and possibly a third in the problematic Pictish language. Goidelic included Primitive Irish, which was spoken in western Scotland (and probably in parts of west Wales and Cornwall). Brittonic languages were spoken south of the Forth and Clyde, separating in western parts during this period into the mutually intelligible languages of Primitive Cornish, Primitive Welsh and Primitive Cumbric (the forerunners of the distinct Cornish, Welsh and Cumbric). Pictish was probably spoken in most of Scotland north of the Forth/Clyde line, except for the west coast; its southern form was Brittonic, but it may have had a different northern form, totally obscure to us now.[6] Conditioned by these linguistic distinctions, it is nowadays conventional, if not entirely rational, to

32. The distribution of languages in Celtic Britain

distinguish three 'peoples' – Irish, British, Pictish – in non-English Britain. There may have been some cultural and ethnic differences which coincided with the linguistic distinctions, but this is very much an open question and one which is difficult to investigate in the absence of adequate source material. Despite my own doubts that there were three distinct peoples, to save confusion I shall use the convention of referring to three population groups (Irish, British and Pictish), while emphasising that the primary meaning of the terms refers to dominant languages, whether or not further cultural differences coincided with the linguistic one. (In fact, strictly, we should refer to the Irish as 'Scots' – the term most frequently used in early medieval sources.)

If the two traditional images are inadequate, what can more positively be suggested? What was happening to these peoples between the fifth and the eighth centuries? There are two kinds of political development that had a lasting significance – migration and the emergence of kings.[7] The fifth and sixth centuries were not only a period of English immigration into eastern and southern England, but a period of Celtic movement too. Some British left Britain and settled on the Continent, especially in France, giving their name (and perhaps their language) to Brittany;[8] others (but not all) moved within the island. More significantly for the future development of Britain, there was movement into Britain from Ireland. This affected at least

Cornwall, Dyfed and Gwynedd (including Anglesey) as well as south-west Scotland, as we know from traces of the Irish language in the place-names of western Britain, from the presence of kings with Irish names in south-west Wales, and from the monuments bearing the Irish script known as ogam. One such monument is the sixth century tombstone from Ivybridge in Devon. Of the two names on the stone, one is inscribed in Latin – *Fanoni Maquirini* – on the face and in ogam along the corner. The other face and corner bear the name *Sagrani*.[9] The Irish movement to British areas probably took place in the late fourth and fifth centuries; for Scotland, on the other hand, there is precise evidence of movement from Ireland in the late sixth century (although it is possible that some Irish leaders were established in Argyll two or three generations earlier).[10] Their movement is of considerable importance for the history of Scotland, since later kings traced their ancestry to the early Irish dynasties.[11] Population movement, therefore, is characteristic of many areas (not all) in the first half of our period: British people moved overseas and perhaps west; Irish people moved into western coastal areas.

33. The Ivybridge Stone

34. The Irish migration to Scotland

The second clear political development – and in many ways the most striking – is that kingdoms were established in 'British' Britain, that is in Wales, the west and the Scottish lowlands. These areas had previously been included within the provinces of Roman Britain, and had therefore been subject to Roman government, although the south and east had been more romanised than the north and west. However, the emergence of kingdoms was as characteristic of romanised as of unromanised parts, and we know of at least fourteen of them. If evidence were less fragmentary we would surely know of more. In one case – Glywysing in south-east Wales – the process of the kingdom's formation can be outlined, as it happened during the seventh century. A warrior called Meurig (of unknown origin, possibly foreign) suddenly appeared in the Chepstow area. He assumed control of the Wye valley, married the king of Ergyng's daughter, then took control of the Vale of Glamorgan and Gower, displacing the Gower king. His grandson Morgan moved throughout south-east Wales, acting as overking to minor kings in north Gwent, and in the Cardiff and Caerleon areas. His great-grandson Ithel established a single, consolidated kingdom of the south east, although the old royal lines survived as aristocratic families in their respective areas.[12]

That pattern was not necessarily typical, and we should expect variety in both origins and development of kingdoms. They ranged

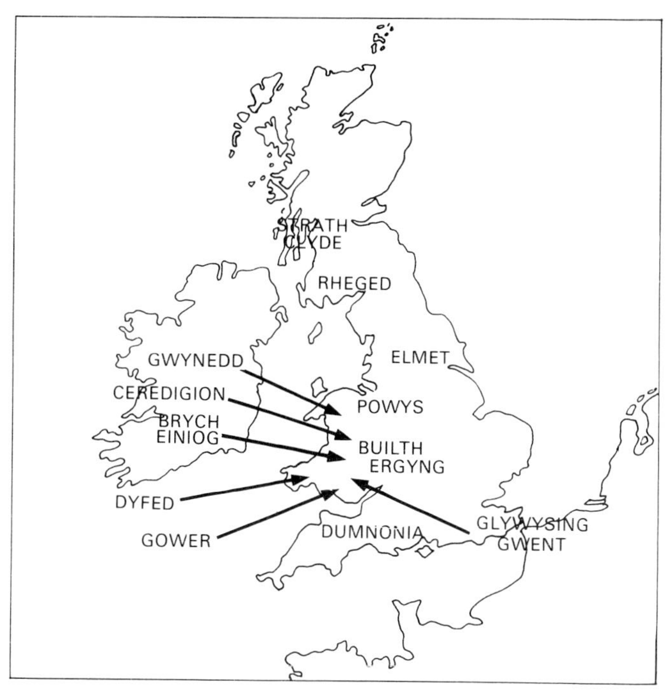


35. The British kingdoms

from a rather large Dumnonia in the south (Cornwall, Devon and probably west Somerset), to a tiny Ergyng (south-west Hereford) and tiny Gower, to a not much larger Elmet (near Leeds), to possibly a huge Rheged (on both sides of the Pennines) and a substantial Strathclyde (focused on the River Clyde).[13] Most of these kingdoms are clearly in evidence by the early sixth century. We must therefore presume that they were created during the migration period of the fifth century, a time of obvious instability. This means that political fragmentation in the Roman provinces was very speedy, irrespective of Anglo-Saxon or Irish settlement. Now the nature of these British kingdoms was such that kings controlled territories rather than tribal groups, doubtless by the use of the warriors who were their companions. When they died they passed on their authority to members of their families, establishing dynasties. They had very little machinery of government – no more than a few agents to do whatever business turned up and very little sense of office or responsibility. They may seem insignificant, but the fact that the kingdoms emerged was to be of considerable importance for the future development of Wales and the west.

Turning from the British to the Picts and Irish, it looks as if the pattern of development among those groups was quite different. We certainly know of Pictish kings from the late sixth century onwards but kingship may well be of much earlier origin, a continuation of an ancient tradition. Whatever the number of Pictish kingdoms at the outset, there seems to have been a single consolidated Pictish kingship by the late eighth century and there are hints that Pictish kings were developing some real machinery of government by that time: there is, for example, a reference to officers of King Nechtan in 729, called *exactatores*, and the name strongly suggests some tax-collecting capacity.[14] In the west of Scotland the early kings, the Dal Riada, came from Ireland. In the late sixth and seventh centuries they raided over a very wide area, possibly from the Orkneys to Anglo-Saxon Northumbria. A single, unitary kingship seems (as in the east) to have emerged by the eighth century, and here too there may have been some institutional development by the seventh century; the text known as *Senchus Fer nAlban* details the military obligations of territories in Argyll – presumably due to the king – and could refer to as early a period as this.[15]

Detail about the activities of kings from all areas is almost entirely confined to warfare; if they did other things we do not hear about them. There was border warfare with the English in British Britain, and a complex pattern of military relationships between Irish, Picts, British and English in southern and central Scotland. However, the English were defeated in 685 and their subsequent withdrawal left Scotland north of the Forth effectively controlled by Pictish and Irish kings, who came into contact with each other increasingly during the eighth century, and whose families sometimes intermarried.[16] In the seventh century, in particular, and not just in Scotland, kings took part in very wide-ranging expeditions, travelling immense distances. Cadwallon of Anglesey ravaged in midland England, Aedan of the Dal Riada in northern Scotland, and maybe a Breton king ruled in Cornwall (or vice versa). This being so, they cannot have had much, if any, contact with their subjects at home.

If kings were fighting, what was happening to other people? It should not be ignored that all three peoples were living through marked changes in their environment. In the former Roman provinces there was contraction in size and deterioration of fabric at urban sites and a lack of repair (and sometimes abandonment) of country houses. Of course, characteristically Roman structures did not disappear (the Welsh cleric Giraldus Cambrensis could comment on the Roman walls of Carmarthen as late as the twelfth century) but their use might well have changed. Roman forts, such as Caerhun in north Wales, became the sites of churches, and the footings of the Roman villa at Llandough near Cardiff were used by monastic builders of the thirteenth century. Some people, probably kings and leaders, began living on hilltop sites in the fifth century, enclosing small areas for

36. The fortress of Dunadd

their protection; this happened from Tintagel on the north coast of Cornwall, to Dinas Powys near Cardiff, to Dinas Emrys near Snowdonia, to Dumbarton, focus of the British kingdom of Strathclyde, and Dunadd, focus of the Dal Riada. Other places – rural and less significant centres of consumption though by no means squalid or uncomfortable – show signs of being inhabited both in the Roman period and beyond, places from Trethurgy in Cornwall to Cefn Graeanog in Gwynedd or the Udal in the Hebrides. Here change or abandonment often came in the seventh rather than the fifth century.

In fact, long-term changes in the settlement pattern may well have been conditioned by large-scale environmental change: the climatic deterioration brought colder, wetter weather that limited productive capacity in higher (and more northern) areas and therefore made the farming of some parts uneconomic. In such cases people had to move to more favourable localities. The entire period from the fourth to the eighth century was probably one of settlement shift – a shift conditioned by fundamental economic determinants such as climate as well as by political and cultural factors such as migration.

Let us now turn from environment to behaviour: what did *non-royal* people do? Some very broad outlines can be indicated for the British in Wales, the west and the Scottish lowlands. British society was a stratified, slave-owning society, in which slavery persisted for longer than was normal in Europe. There was differentiation between rich and poor and between superior and inferior; at the least there was an aristocracy, a slave group (most would have been born slaves, although it is known that a Saxon woman formed part of the payment handed over in a sale in south-east Wales in about 740),[17] and a stratum of those who were in neither category. There were probably finer distinctions that this. It is quite likely that one of the additional strata was of tied tenants. Some proportion of the agrarian labour force was hereditarily bound: they were born tenants and obliged to remain such, returning at least an annual render to their landlords. This undoubtedly limited their personal freedom for their powers of negotiation were effectively none, although they were not *themselves* chattels, as slaves were, and there are no suggestions that they were bound to perform labour services for their landlords. In this they seem to have been less badly off than their English and continental counterparts.

Some characteristics of the landlord group are also apparent. It was the landlords, clerical and monastic as well as lay, who conducted local business, saw to the regulation of transactions and settlement of disputes. In south-east Wales, they were known as 'elders' and were clearly small farmers rather than great aristocrats. Public meetings drew people from a radius of about twenty-four kilometres, people who had property in that area but not much more. One record of dispute settlement nicely demonstrates the role of elders. It was written on a page of the Lichfield Gospels, for safe keeping, when the Gospels were at Llandeilo Fawr (not far from Carmarthen) in the eighth or ninth century:

> Tudfwlch the son of Llywyd and the son-in-law of Tudri arose to claim 'Tir Telych', which was in the hand of Elcu the son of Gelli and the tribe of Idwared. They disputed long about it; in the end they disjudge Tudri's son-in-law by law. The goodmen [elders] said to each other, 'Let us make peace'. Elcu gave afterwards a horse, three cows, three newly-calved cows, only in order that there might not be hatred between them from the ruling afterwards till the Day of Judgement . . . Tudfwlch and his kin will not want it for ever and ever.[18] [A list of witnesses and religious sanction follows.]

The last sentence reminds us of the importance of family bonds, for Tudfwlch's family was affected by this settlement.

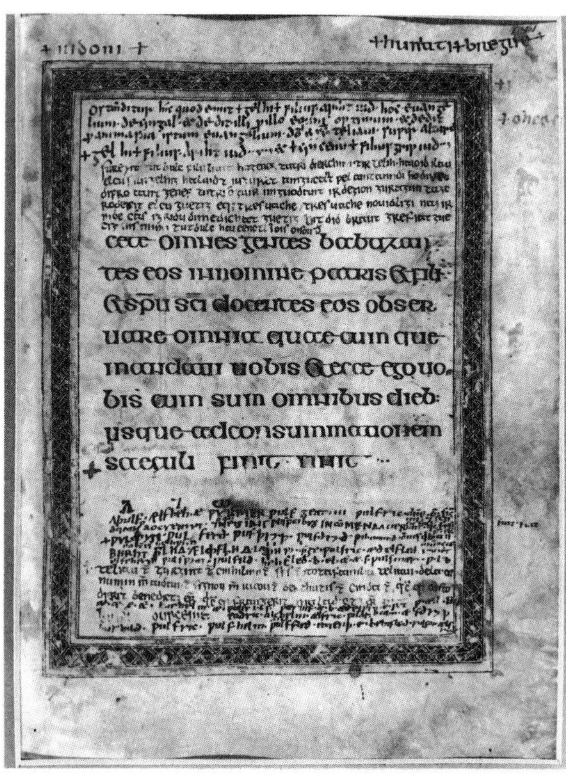

37, 38. Legal records copied into the Lichfeld Gospels

There is other evidence on this subject. The wider family, the kindred, would have had some role in relation to property, marriage and assault; that is, uncles and cousins would have been involved in the transmission of property in some circumstances and in the arrangement of marriages, and uncles and cousins would have been responsible for damage caused by one of their kin and would have received compensation for damage done to them. However, this does not mean that everything was done with second cousins and great-grandfather taking part. The nuclear family seems to have been the basic residential group, with a tight relationship which took precedence over others. St Samson's mother looked after the young child and was even concerned about his play, and the wife of Bishop Bivatigos was very precious to him, as a tombstone from Llantrisant, Anglesey, records.[19] In fact family connections, through the alliances created by marriage, were a major element in ensuring social stability (although the pattern of kindred alliances was increasingly complicated by attempts of the church to interfere in marriage practice).[20]

Overall, social and economic support was largely provided by kindred, and also lordship, structures. However, there is no evidence to suggest that these mechanisms of social support extended to slaves and tied tenants (although economic support obviously did). Their personal security seems to have been a fragile thing and there is no evidence of any machinery adequate to support such individuals in times of difficulty.

Outside British areas of Britain, among the Picts and Irish, it is even more difficult to perceive social structures at this very early period. Virtually nothing can be said about Pictish society, although it is believed that matrilineal succession was usual in the royal family. This means that kings were selected from the sons of royal women, not royal men; hence, a king's nephew or brother would tend to succeed him, rather than his son.[21] There is, however, no reason to suppose this inheritance practice extended to the whole of society.

A possible source of information about Pictish life could be the many symbol stones of this period – quite large monuments, carved with curious and intricate designs, but with virtually no clues to meaning, apart from some Christian associations and the portrayal of warrior groups. All sorts of imaginative attempts have been made to fashion social structures from these pictures: at present they remain ingenious but untestable.[22]

More positively, the *Life of Columba* written by Adomnan, abbot of Iona off the west coast of Scotland, in about 700, allows a few glimpses into Scottish society, although it is not always possible to

39. Pictish symbol stone

distinguish between Irish and Pictish elements. Much of it, however, is about the Irish. There are the same indications of social stratification, of the strength of the nuclear family complemented by the role of the wider kindred, of slaves and tied tenants, and of military lordship, as there are in British areas.[23]

Clearly, therefore, it would not be correct to suppose that outside the area of Anglo-Saxon settlement there was one pan-Celtic society in Britain; and if Ireland were included in the picture the differences would be yet more strongly marked. At the very least there were significant differences between Irish, Pictish and British areas. There were major political and environmental differences between one region and another (from county to county in modern terms), and if there were more detailed early texts we could shade in the different operation of kinship and lordship structures and the differing definitions of noble and non-noble strata, as we moved from place to place. The traditional images with which I began – saints and heroes – have a grain of truth in them, but it is only a grain. Heroic society is about leaders and aristocrats, and relates to border areas; it is not about the mass of the population and it is not about a large part of Britain. Sainthood there may well have been. Indeed, the spread of Christianity must constitute one of the greatest social changes of this period, in all areas. This is a change which affected not only ritual practice such as burial and birth customs, but also economic fundamentals. Saints received endowments; churches and monasteries and their communities became landowners, very rapidly in the late sixth, seventh and eighth centuries. So the tenant population acquired new kinds of landlords; and they often acquired fewer, and therefore richer, landlords. The stronger images are of small-scale, inward-looking, agrarian societies, with little consciousness of a wider world; kings and their warbands impinged little on everyday life but the new monastic landlords were nearer at home and their interests were in agrarian exploitation.

Let me end with some alternative images to set against the romantic ones with which I began. First, from Adomnan's *Life of Columba*:

> But concerning a certain very niggardly rich man . . . who had slighted Saint Columba, and did not receive him as a guest, [the saint] on the contrary, pronounced this prophetic doom: 'The riches of that greedy man, who has spurned Christ in pilgrim guests, will from this day be gradually diminished, and will be reduced to nothing. And he himself will be a beggar . . . And he will die, struck with an axe by one of his enemies, in the trench of a threshing-floor.' All these things concerning each were completely fulfilled.[24]

And another piece written in the margins of the Lichfield Gospels, then known as St Teilo's Gospels, right at the end of our period:

> It is necessary to inscribe some letters to the effect that the four sons of Bleddri . . . have given freedom to Bleiddud son of Sulien and his seed for ever, for a price: and this is the confirmation that he gave four pounds and eight ounces [of silver] for his freedom. [It was done] in front of law-worthy witnesses, Rhiwallon . . . Arthan son of Cimulch . . . Bishop Nobis . . . Dubrinus, Cuhelyn the bishop's son. . . . Whoever shall preserve this decree of freedom for Bleiddud and his seed shall be blessed: he who does not preserve it shall be cursed by God and by Teilo, in whose Gospels it is written.[25]

The saint was a man of power; he knew it, and used it. The hero needed the slave if he was to indulge in feasting and fighting. And the getting of food absorbed most people most of the time.

## Further reading

A.O. and M.O. Anderson (eds), *Adomnan's Life of Columba* (London, 1961); F.J. Byrne, *Irish Kings and High-Kings* (London, 1973); W. Davies, *Wales in the Early Middle Ages* (Leicester, 1982); K.H. Jackson, *The Gododdin* (Edinburgh, 1969); S.M. Pearce, *The Kingdom of Dumnonia* (Padstow, 1978); C. Thomas, *Christianity in Roman Britain to* AD500 (London, 1981).

CHAPTER SIX

# The Christian Connection

Liam de Paor

The civilisation of Europe has been shaped for nearly two thousand years by the powerful force of the Christian religion in its various forms and manifestations. In Britain too this great social, cultural, intellectual – and spiritual – force has permeated the country's life for centuries. But Britain was not converted to Christianity in one simple missionary endeavour. No less than three distinct major enterprises were involved. This gave rise to a complex culture that was ultimately to achieve considerable unity of belief and a measure of harmony and civilisation long before political unity came to Britain.

The first introduction of Christianity had taken place in the centuries of Roman rule. The Gospel message was brought from the Near East by the merchants, slaves, soldiers and administrators who passed ceaselessly on the roads and seaways of the empire. The Christian message of salvation was competing successfully not only with belief in the old Celtic gods of the Britons, but also with other exotic salvation-religions brought from Egypt, Persia and other parts through the Roman communication network. By the end of the fourth century, the Christian Church had been established in Roman Britain in some form for at least two hundred years.[1] Beyond Hadrian's Wall, to the north, were the Picts, still pagan at the end of the fourth century, and outside the empire. To the west, across the sea, were the Irish, also mostly pagan, and of Celtic speech. They still lived in tribally organised Iron Age societies, unconquered by Rome. To the east, beyond the North Sea, were warlike German tribes, again pagan, living outside the imperial borders. All of these had begun to raid Roman Britain for valuables and slaves. In the fifth century, a society which was still incompletely Christianised was beset on three sides by pagan enemies. The raiders began to settle in increasing numbers both in the west and in the east, taking land for themselves. Irish settlement was on a fairly small scale on the Welsh coast, but more extensive in western Scotland.

But in southern and eastern Britain the pagan Anglo-Saxons established their own society and economy, which contrasted sharply with that of the Christianised Britons who still occupied the western and central regions. The organised Christian Church survived among the Britons; it disappeared in the Anglo-Saxon areas. It seems that among the British provinces struggling for their survival against these pressures, Christianity not only survived but continued to expand. In the west, the British dialects of the ordinary people completely replaced the Latin of the ruling classes for general purposes, and these dialects survive as modern Welsh. However, Latin continued as the language of the church. It is probable that in Britain, as elsewhere at this date, many of the church leaders may have been drawn from the administrative class, trained in Roman schools. They by no means confined their leadership to church matters, but regularly concerned themselves with such affairs as the distribution of food supplies or the mustering of defences against barbarian attack.

Even while Christianity was being wiped out in eastern Britain, Christians seem to have regrouped in the west and to have organised the church among the increasing number of Christians to be found among the barbarians beyond the frontiers. This occurred especially in the buffer states between the empire and the barbarians, such as Strathclyde and the lands of the southern Picts. There were also Christian communities in southern and eastern Ireland, in coastal areas that had been visited for centuries by traders from Roman Gaul and Britain.

Two new developments affected the British church in this time of turmoil. One was the arrival of a new enthusiasm from the East: the practice of monasticism. This was a movement of total withdrawal from the world. People retired into desert or remote places to live celibate lives of prayer and fasting, following a rule of discipline laid down by some holy person. The custom was already established in Gaul, and there is some evidence of its introduction to Britain at about this time. A Christian settlement of the fifth century at Tintagel, Cornwall, may have been an early monastery.[2]

The other development was the emergence in Britain of a 'heresy' or unorthodox teaching, known as Pelagianism after its founder, Pelagius. Earlier, while there had been fierce controversies in the Christian Church concerning what exactly it was that Christians should believe, Britain had been reported to be quite orthodox. But the new heresy led to several interventions from the churches of Gaul acting in consultation with the church in Rome, where the popes took over the direction of the effort to restore orthodoxy.

40. Tintagel

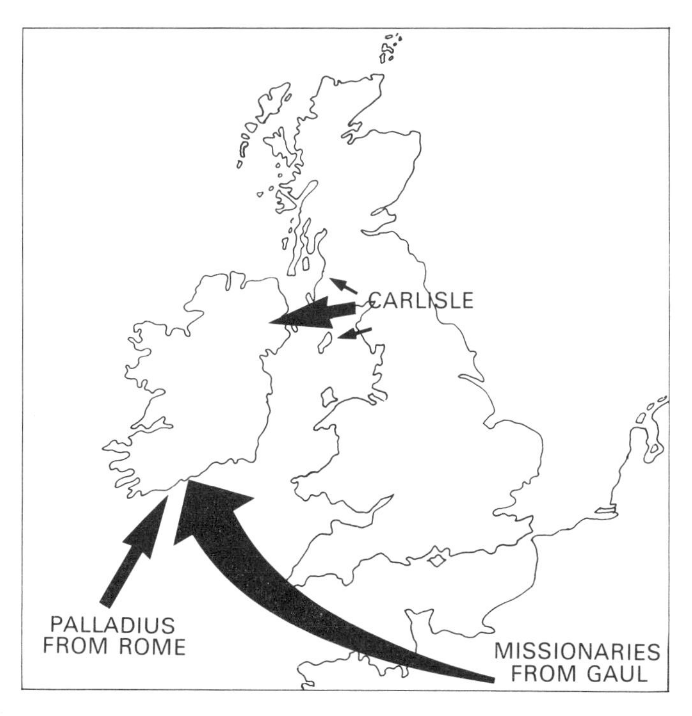


41. The evangelisation of Ireland

An important result was the organisation of missions in Ireland. This began when Pope Celestine consecrated the deacon Palladius and sent him in 431 to be the first bishop of the Irish Christian communities. It is likely that this was intended to forestall the spread of Pelagianism outside Roman Britain.[3] It suggests that, for the church in Gaul, Ireland was to be reckoned an extension of its British responsibilities. Many other Gaulish bishops were to work in Ireland in the fifth century, bringing the Christian faith into the interior.

The Britons themselves sponsored the extension of their church organisation beyond the imperial frontiers. It was probably from Carlisle that bishops – St Nynia, St Patrick and St Maughold[4] – were sent to south-west Scotland, north-east Ireland and the Isle of Man. Most of this expansive activity took place after the Romans had left the Britons to their own devices. There seems to have been a brief period of some fifty years of comparative stability – perhaps even some prosperity – in the decades after 500 during which the Romano-British church had time and opportunity to strengthen its position.

However, the animosity between the two peoples, Celtic Britons and the invading Germanic Anglo-Saxons, went so deep that no British attempt to convert their pagan adversaries to Christianity is known. In spite of the warfare and of the breakdown of order, not only in Britain but also in Gaul, the Roman and Gaulish church continued to maintain contact with western Britain. Shortly after the middle of the century, for example, it seems that the British accepted from the bishop of Rome a revised method of calculating the dates of the movable festival of Easter.

From 550 onwards, the renewed expansion of the Anglo-Saxon settlement provoked a major collapse of British political culture and some demoralisation in the church. At the same time, the monastic movement came to dominate church organisations, and there were necessarily realignments in both the British and the Irish churches. With the British defeats and retreats towards the highland refuges of the west, the Irish pupils, not their British teachers, began to take the initiative in church matters.

Here began the second distinct mission to convert mainland Britain to Christianity, this time led by Celtic monks. Monasteries of the eastern type now became the chief Christian centres of the west. The best preserved is off the south-west coast of Ireland, the Skelling Rock, about twelve kilometres from the County Kerry mainland. It is not quite typical, since in this timberless situation its buildings are of stone, not wood, and since its community plainly wanted more than most to be remote and alone. There are six huts here, with a couple of tiny oratories or chapels. Each hut, whose interior measured about four square metres, would have housed two or three monks.

42. Skelling Rock
43. Skelling Monastery

Establishments such as these were modelled on those of western Britain; they rapidly became extremely numerous in Ireland.[5]

The monks followed rules of extreme austerity, attempting to discipline body, mind and spirit. In Irish society of the time, ties of kinship were of overwhelming legal, social, and therefore psychological importance. Separation from kin was a severe penance. Total separation, from kin and homeland, was the greatest deprivation. After the middle of the sixth century, Irish monks, seeking this ultimate renunciation, began to leave Ireland in some numbers. One of these migrations was to have important consequences in Britain.

In 563, the priest Columba, born Cremthann, a member of the inner kin-group of the most powerful royal dynasty of the northern half of Ireland, sailed to western Scotland with some companions. He founded a monastery on Iona, a little island off the larger island of Mull. This brought him just beyond the northern limit of the colonial kingdom established in Scotland by the east Ulster kingdom of Dal Riada, rivals of Columba's own dynasty. To certify his right to the island, Columba travelled up the Great Glen to meet Brude, the king of the Picts, whom he converted to Christianity. In the following years many further monasteries were to be founded in Scotland and Ireland; from Iona many hermits went, as Columba's biographer puts it 'to seek a solitude in the pathless sea'.[6]

From the start, Iona also played its part in the political realignment of Scotland, establishing a scriptorium for the copying of manuscripts, influencing the counsels of kings, and becoming a safe repository of records and chronicles. In 574 Columba himself solemnly anointed and inaugurated Aidan as king of Dal Riada – an act of great political significance. Within a couple of generations, Iona was the head and centre of a federation of monasteries in Britain and Ireland, all of which followed the rule of Columba and were responsible and subordinate to his successor on the island.

For a number of generations, the rulers of the federation, Columba's successors, were members of the same royal kin-group (whose centre was in Donegal) and so commanded great influence in the politics of the north. The island monastery was closely in touch with the wider world, and developments – for example, in the eastern church, in the distant Byzantine Empire – were perhaps more quickly reflected there than anywhere else in the west.

Meanwhile, throughout the second half of the sixth century, the Anglo-Saxon expansion continued spreading over all of lowland Britain, overwhelming not only the culture of the Britons but also the Christianity which that culture had accepted. This was the position when a carefully prepared plan for the recovery of England (as we may now begin to call that country) was put into effect by Pope

Gregory the Great. Gregory belonged by blood, training and instinct to the old Roman ruling class. His Rome, however, was a shadow of its former imperial self. No emperor had ruled there for more than a hundred years. He had been Prefect of Rome as a young man, then became a monk following the rule of St Benedict, and gained administrative and diplomatic experience in the papal service before becoming pope himself. He envisaged a restoration of the western Roman Empire; but in his vision the new legions would be priests and monks. The Franks who had overrun Gaul were Christian by now; the Anglo-Saxons who occupied what had been Roman Britain were pagan. Gregory proposed their conversion. This was the third great mission to convert the peoples of Britain.

Gregory's officials consulted the old imperial records and the plan of conversion was based, not on the existing division of Britain into warring Anglo-Saxon and other petty kingdoms, but on a restoration of the older Roman administrative divisions. Bishops were to be appointed to these, with metropolitans in London and York, and twelve other bishops in each of these provinces. In practice, this plan had to be modified to fit in with the political realities of Britain at the time.

A monk called Augustine, provost of the Benedictine monastery in Rome where Gregory had been trained, was chosen to carry out the enterprise. He was supplied with numerous letters to clerics and rulers along the way, and was sent with a band of monks to England in 596. Augustine and his monks appear to have been faint-hearted about their hazardous and difficult mission, but they were not permitted to flinch, and in due course they arrived, like the first Roman legions more than five centuries earlier, on the coast of Kent.

The king of Kent, Ethelbert, was married to a Frankish princess who was a Christian. She had a Frankish bishop as her chaplain, and had restored to use an old Christian church at Canterbury. Ethelbert himself, however, was a pagan, and was surrounded by priests and retainers who had a vested interest in the old pagan beliefs.

Ethelbert and Augustine met in the open air, the monks carrying a silver cross and an image of Christ painted on wood.[7] Generally speaking, in such confrontations, whether with the old Celtic or the old Germanic religions, Christianity had considerable advantages. First, it carried with it the great prestige of Roman civilisation, backed since the time of Constantine by the power of the state. And even those barbarians who had contributed to the decline of Rome in the west held the empire in awe and admiration. But by now the Christian faith also offered a coherent and systematic body of doctrine, moulded by Hellenistic philosophy, which had much more appeal to the educated or intelligent mind than had the amorphous pantheons of gods and goddesses who were personifications of natural forces or spirits of places, trees, rocks or pools. For uneducated peasants or workers, it had another appeal, that summed up in Marx's phrase, 'the opium of the people': it offered consolation for the hardship of their lives. It promised personal salvation and the joys of paradise in an afterlife.

Bede sums this up well. In his account of the conversion of another Anglo-Saxon ruler, one of the king's advisers says:

> When we compare the present life of man on earth with that time of which we have no knowledge, it seems to me like the swift flight of a single sparrow through the banqueting hall. . . . This sparrow flies swiftly in through one door of the hall, and out through another. While he is inside, he is safe from the winter storms, but after a few moments of comfort, he vanishes from sight into the wintry world from which he came. . . .[8]

Christianity offered a comforting certainty to replace this austere, if touching, image of human life. But there was of course some resistance to it, and the quickest way to change these comparatively simple societies was through the ruler – who commanded not only military power but also to some extent unseen forces of the other world – being a sacral person descended from a god.

In Kent, King Ethelbert's conversion was not immediate; he was baptised probably in 601. And Pope Gregory's grand design proceeded slowly. Augustine never established himself in London as was originally intended; he remained at Canterbury, which was to become the metropolitan see of the south. Within a few years he sent to Rome for more helpers. Some of these became bishops of neighbouring centres, including London. One of Gregory's instructions on prudent missionary procedures is interesting: 'The idols are to be destroyed, but the temples are to be aspersed, altars set up in them, and relics deposited there.'[9] It is probable that in this way several Christian stone churches of the Roman period, converted after the Saxon invasion to pagan use, were now converted back to Christian worship. When Augustine died, sometime in the first decade of the seventh century, he left an established and slowly expanding church in the south-east corner of England.

There was one major problem which Augustine could not overcome: the British bishops refused to acknowledge his authority. His mission represented a direct reassertion of Roman authority in Britain. But the Christian churches which had weathered the storms of the previous two centuries were not prepared to give way readily to this new order. Besides, Augustine's church was firmly associated with the Anglo-Saxons, and between them on the one hand and the Britons on the other, there was still continuing warfare.

After the death of Ethelbert, the mission passed through a very difficult period. But an opportunity to expand northwards came when Ethelbert's daughter, a Christian, married Edwin, king of the Anglian territory of Northumbria. One of Augustine's companions, Paulinus, was consecrated bishop and travelled with Ethelbert's daughter to the north. In 626 Edwin accepted baptism, and as he was at that time the most powerful English ruler, his example was followed by many. Edwin was succeeded in the kingship of Northumbria by Oswald, who had been educated in Irish monastic schools, both in Ireland and Iona. As soon as he had established himself as the ruler of Northumbria, he sent to distant Iona for monks to come and help re-establish Christianity in his kingdom. Bede tells us that on the site of Heavenfield – where Oswald defeated his chief enemy, Cadwallon – he set up a wooden cross before the battle. This idea he may well have acquired from the Irish monks of Iona, where the ancient stone crosses

45. Celtic crosses on Iona

are derived from wooden prototypes.

From Iona came the monk Aidan, with a number of companions, bringing the monastic culture of the Atlantic to the shores of the North Sea. They settled on the island of Lindisfarne and were followed by reinforcements from Iona, who founded other churches and monasteries. These carried on with enthusiasm the work of preaching the Gospel to the Anglians.

By this date, the middle of the seventh century, the traditions of Roman learning and culture which had been brought to the British and the Irish and had been preserved by them since the twilight of the Roman Empire, had blended with older traditions rooted in a remote Celtic past. The result now was the flowering of a distinctive literature, matched by brilliant productions in metalworking, stone sculpture and manuscript painting. In the north these interacted with the equally brilliant decorative and craft traditions of the Anglo-Saxons. The Anglo-Saxons in turn began to acquire literacy through Christianity and to produce their own literature.

However, the Roman and the Celtic concepts of ecclesiastical order were not wholly compatible, and there were difficulties. It was in the field of organisation, and in connexion with questions of authority, that discrepancies came to a crisis. The question of the authority of Canterbury remained unresolved. The churches of the west and north, claiming antiquity and tradition, were not willing to yield their claim to the new mission. The Irish missionary Columbanus, working in Gaul, had expressed this point of view at the beginning of the century in letters to popes of the time; he enjoined one of them to follow 'the hundred and fifty authorities of the Council of Constantinople, who decreed that churches of God planted in pagan nations, should live by their own laws, as they had been instructed by their fathers'. He wrote to Pope Boniface that the 'inhabitants of the world's edge, are disciples of Saints Peter and Paul', and that 'the Catholic faith, as it was delivered by you first, who are successors of the holy apostles, is maintained unbroken'.[10]

The conflict between the new mission in Kent and the older established churches in Britain was not centred around doctrine. But quite apart from the refusal of the British churches to accept Rome's authority, there was also great lack of uniformity in custom and practice. In particular, differences in the methods of calculating the dates of Easter from year to year led to anomalies, this major Christian festival being celebrated on one Sunday in some parts of Britain and on a different Sunday in others. In Northumbria Oswiu celebrated Easter according to the Iona calendar; his Kentish queen with her clergy celebrated it according to the Roman, or Canterbury, calendar.

It was in Northumbria that the major confrontation between the two systems took place, in 663. The king, Oswiu, presided at a meeting at Whitby at which the differences in practice between the church of Canterbury, and the Irish and British churches were argued out, with the result that Canterbury prevailed. Our chief account of this meeting comes from Bede, writing about half a century later. He perhaps exaggerates the importance of some of the technicalities discussed – he had strong feelings on the matter in favour of the Canterbury view – but the decision did have a considerable effect on Northumbria. Most of the Irish withdrew from Lindisfarne to Ireland, or back to Scotland, leaving the field to their opponents.

The meeting at Whitby was to set the pattern for the church in Britain which had been divided between two Christian traditions. Full unity was to take time, but by bringing the dominant English kingdom of the time over to Canterbury the Whitby meeting was to prove crucial. The victory was won probably because it was seen by the secular rulers to bring the church in Britain into line with continental practice. Although the merits of the Celtic churches were acknowledged, their customs were seen to be extravagant and eccentric. The sober practicality of the Benedictine form of monasticism and the methodical organisation now supervised from Rome had greater appeal, especially to kings and rulers.

The process of union was spread over a series of conferences and agreements between the two traditions, but it was given a great impetus by an appointment which had the effect almost of a new mission from Rome. Theodore of Tarsus, an elderly, widely experienced, highly cultivated Greek, was appointed archbishop of Canterbury, where he arrived in 669. He was a man of great learning and administrative ability, and he was to survive as archbishop for more than twenty years. In that period, he reorganised and revitalised the church. He had protégés such as Benedict Biscop, a Northumbrian who founded and endowed many monasteries and schools. He brought artists and builders and other craftsmen from Italy, imported manuscripts and generally encouraged the reintroduction of Roman civilisation. In the north and west in particular, this blended with the cultural revival already occurring, to produce what has been called the golden age of the English church, in the eighth century. It was a Christian golden age, too, for Scotland and Ireland.

The blend of Roman, Celtic and Anglo-Saxon is exemplified in that remarkable work of sculpture, the cross of Ruthwell, erected in about AD700, which is inscribed in runes with a version of the poem known as the *Dream of the Rood*. The cross speaks:

> Unclothed himself God almighty when he would mount his cross, courageous in the sight of all men . . . I durst not bend. Men mocked us both together. I was bedewed with blood. . . .[11]

It is exemplified too in the pages of great Gospel-books, such as that of Lindisfarne, whose majestic, mysteriously ornamented pages drew

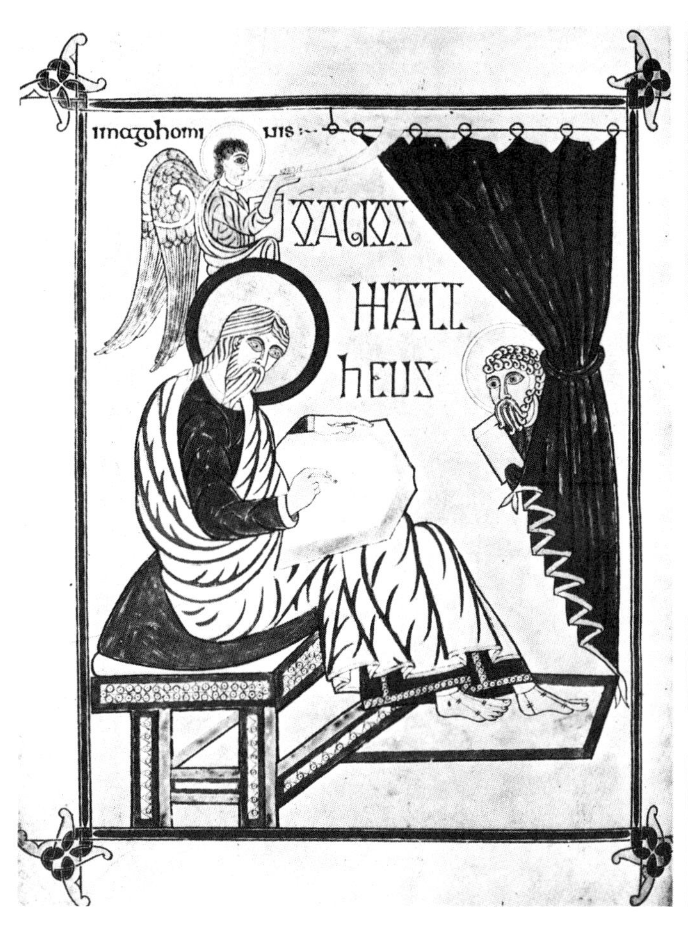

46. A page from the Book of Lindisfarne

47. The Ruthwell Cross

on the cultural history of the different peoples who, through conversion to a common belief and through the restraints which it attempted to impose on their enmities, began to create a shared culture.

In England one of its most remarkable ornaments was Bede. He was a product of the twin monasteries of Wearmouth and Jarrow, founded by Benedict Biscop, which possessed the best library, it was said, outside Italy. Bede wrote many learned works, in particular the history of the English church, a history centred on the Gregorian mission and celebrating the imposition of Roman order and uniformity. He gives credit, however, to the Celtic tradition. Writing about the year 730 he says:

> At the present time there are in Britain, in harmony with the five books of the divine law, five languages and four nations – English, British, Irish and Picts. Each has its own language; but all are united

> in the study of God's truth by the fifth – Latin – which has become a common medium through the study of the scriptures.[12]

The enthusiasm, gentleness and austerity of the Celtic founders had made a deep impression on the north, which remained long after the new order had displaced their tradition. In Scotland, Columba in particular was revered and his relic honoured. In Northumbria special affection continued for Cuthbert, a saint of the Celtic tradition, whose figured coffin and pectoral cross have survived the centuries because of the care bestowed on them.

By the eighth century Britain was, by and large, a Christian land. The church entered more and more fully into the life of society as a whole. It took over the pagan and warlike institutions of kingship and gave it a special Christian – and undoubtedly more civilised – meaning, by adapting the traditions surrounding the sacred person of the god-descended king to the models of biblical kingship and priesthood. Columba, as we saw, anointed Aidan king of the Dal Riada – the first such occasion we know of in the West – and the ceremonials of anointing, crowning and enthroning, which Christianised pagan rituals, were intended to give authority and dignity and to assist the process of political centralisation and state creation. Church and state went hand in hand in this process whose rituals have survived in Britain to the present day.

## Further reading

A.O. and M.O. Anderson (eds), *Adomnan's Life of Columba* (London, 1961); M. Deanesly, *The Pre-Conquest Church in England* (London, 1961); S.M. Pearce, *The Early Church in Western Britain and Ireland* (London, 1982); C. Thomas, *Christianity in Roman Britain to AD500* (London, 1981).

CHAPTER SEVEN

# The Viking Nation

## Klavs Randsborg

In June 793 a band of heathen Norsemen landed on the east coast of England and sacked the monastery at Lindisfarne. The Vikings who were to influence, and even dominate, life in Europe for the next two hundred and fifty years, had made their first raid on Britain. Who were these previously little-known Norsemen? Why did they suddenly become so important? What accounts for their large-scale raids on Britain?

The Vikings were the Norwegians, Danes and Swedes, inhabitants of the major part of what we now know as Scandinavia. They shared, with some regional variations, a common culture and language. Scandinavia was on the edge of European development until, in a few decades, the Vikings changed from a marginal people to traders and raiders, lords and settlers. Their reach extended from America to Asia and spanned the course of two great ages of expansion between AD800 and 1050, known to us as the Viking Ages.

In dealing with the archaeological and historical evidence about the Vikings, quite a few scholars have been tempted to rely on the vivid descriptions of bloodthirsty Norsemen from contemporary sources such as the *Anglo-Saxon Chronicle*.[1] But recent archaeological research shows us that the Viking expansion was much more complicated than this.[2] To understand the dramatic events that contemporaries recorded we need to look deep into Viking society and the changes it underwent during these two and a half centuries. In the Viking Ages, the Scandinavian north played a crucial part in the world economy, and this new role prompted great social change within the Scandinavian societies themselves. There was actually a two-fold development: first in the relations of Scandinavia with the rest of the world, then within the Scandinavian societies themselves. This is the key to understanding the Vikings and their impact on Europe.

48. Viking trade routes

Let us begin by looking at the external economic factors during the period of expansion between 800 and 950, the first Viking Age. This was the period first of expanding trade to every corner of the known world, then of raid, and finally of renewed trade.

At the end of the eighth century international trade was transformed.[3] In the 780s, a trade route was established that linked, for the first time, Scandinavia and the Middle East on a fairly regular basis. Viking ships bearing iron, furs and especially slaves travelled along the broad, easily navigated rivers of central Russia, such as the Dnieper and, most important, the Volga, to the trading cities at their estuaries, such as Itil on the Caspian Sea. Here the Vikings met Jewish and Muslim traders who in turn were opening up trade to China. These routes ran via Rayy (later Teheran) and Baghdad – gateways to India, China and the Far East – by sea through the Persian Gulf and by land along the ancient silk roads. From the Near East, other routes stretched south down the east coast of Africa, and west into the Mediterranean, where the Vikings were already trading via the Black Sea and Byzantium. Although Scandinavia had been part of the European trading network, it had never before been drawn into a world economic system of trade and politics stretching as far as China. The profits from this trade led to a massive injection of cash into the underdeveloped tribal economies of Scandinavia. In around 800, Islamic silver flowed through Russia into Scandinavia and no doubt from there into Western Europe. It has even been suggested that this was the economic basis for the so-called Carolingian renaissance, the remarkable cultural development that flowered in the court of the Frankish emperor, Charlemagne. The petty Scandinavian courts also received exotic goods such as silk and peacocks from the distant lands along the trade routes, as did other rulers. Haroun-ar-Rashid, for example, the famous Caliph of Baghdad in *The Arabian Nights*, sent an elephant to the Frankish Emperor, Charlemagne. (The poor animal actually died of influenza when it was brought north to participate in fighting against the Danes.) Although the role of the north in the eastern trade was crucial, the arrival of the elephant shows that other routes were open. However, it remains true that in a very short time around 800, the Norsemen became actively and peaceably engaged in the world around them. Incidents such as the sack of the Lindisfarne monastery in 793 were still rare.

This international trade network collapsed in the second quarter of the ninth century due to economic recession, social unrest and war. For instance, in Mesopotamia, the centre of the Islamic world, the population of the fertile flood plain dropped to only a fragment of its previous size.[4] In Russia, warring and migrations by Magyars and other peoples unsettled a wide area, and communication was broken

49. The Gokstad ship

between the Baltic and Islamic worlds. This had a very significant effect on Viking society, accustomed as it had been to the benefits of a slowly growing trade throughout the eighth century, followed by the very profitable 'eastern adventure'. The kings and the upper classes had acquired new standards of living and had expanded their political and military power, which the end of this profitable trade inevitably threatened. To secure their position they organised expeditions to look for trade and wealth along the ancient trade routes. But the expeditions quickly turned into raiding parties in the hope that plunder could replace trade as a source of income. Here began the terrifying raids of the late ninth century, so vividly recorded by contemporaries. In the *Anglo-Saxon Chronicle*, for example, there are descriptions of Danes speeding along, much like modern commandos, in their superb longships. These craft could enter even small rivers, as their draught was only one metre, yet could withstand waves and storms on the high seas. They were very fast, whether under sail or being rowed by their crews of some forty men. Compared to the size of the crew, however, these narrow ships, displacing less than ten tons, held only a small cargo and were not suitable for the bulk trade in which the Vikings had previously been interested.[5]

Viking armies led by warrior kings roamed abroad for years, wintering in the foreign countries they raided. This resulted in the political domination of large areas of England and France by the Norsemen; at the same time there was large-scale settlement, first by the armies, later by groups of Scandinavians frustrated by the disappearance of the wealth of the earlier period and thus finding it difficult to fulfil their ambitions and expectations at home.

The Danes were not the only people to move out of Scandinavia under the pressure of social and economic circumstances. By the beginning of the Viking Age, the Norwegians had already landed in Scotland, where they established themselves on the northern isles and the Hebrides. In the ninth century, the Vikings seized the uninhabited Faroe Islands and Iceland, and at the very end of the Viking Age, they colonised Greenland's southern tip. A few explorers extended the boundaries of the then known world when they reached the coast of North America and founded a short-lived settlement at L'Anse aux Meadows in Newfoundland.[6]

Ironically, the main body of settlement in the North Atlantic may well have been Celtic slaves under their Norwegian masters. The percentages of the main blood-types in the present-day Icelandic population are identical to those of Ireland, but significantly different to those of the present-day Norwegian or, for that matter, Danish populations.[7] This shows how important it is not to confuse Scandinavian lordship with pure Scandinavian settlement.

To sum up at this point: in the first Viking Age the raids were freelance operations which rose to a peak between 860 and 890, and were followed by settlement. The raids on the West were a response to falling trade, first and foremost with the East. When the Scandinavians were able to reopen the routes to the Near East after 890, the raids died away, ceasing entirely by the mid-tenth century. Why did this happen?

The key to the whole system might well be the new Samanid Empire in Central Asia, based around the fabled cities of Samarkand and Bukhara in Turkestan.[8] This trading dynasty occupied a position at the very crossroads between Europe, the Near East and the Far East. In addition, it controlled some extremely rich silver mines. Once again, large amounts of Islamic silver, this time from Afghanistan and Turkestan, flowed into Scandinavia. Some Islamic merchants and diplomatic missions reached as far as the middle Volga where they came in contact with Vikings trading fur and slaves, while the Vikings themselves sometimes penetrated as far as Baghdad. However, this prosperity endured for only a few decades. In about 950, the Samanid dynasty lost control of all the important trading centres, including Teheran, which was conquered by another Muslim dynasty. The result was that the network of trade could no longer be maintained and so the second wave of Viking trade with the East collapsed. There were far-reaching consequences. For example, the major trading port at Birka, near Stockholm in Sweden, which did survive the first decline (in spite of its dependence on the Russian trade) now crumbled and never rose again.

This situation paralleled the crisis of the first Viking Age. But now, at the beginning of the second Viking Age, we do not see the same response. The collapse of trade did *not* at once give way to raids.[9] In fact, it was some time before the raids began again (in around 990) and when they did, it was on an entirely different scale. These were huge affairs conducted by a large naval force under a strong king who was in control of a secure base at home. Also, by this time Denmark was the most important nation in Scandinavia, expanding at the expense of its neighbours, Norway and Sweden. The Danes organised the great raids and England – one of the wealthiest nations in Western Europe – bore the brunt of the attack. This pattern is entirely different to that of the first Viking Age. To explain the reason for this, we must turn to the nature of Viking society itself and the changes that took place there between the first and second Viking Ages. Denmark in particular furnishes a very good example of the ways in which these changes transformed Scandinavian society. During the first Viking Age, Denmark was dotted with villages and hamlets which had streets and greens. The farms were large, and situated on spacious crofts

50. The fortified wall and harbour at Birka

surrounded by palisades. The main building was a solid wooden longhouse with room for the family, animals, a barn and some storage. Around it were smaller houses, mainly for storage, with some additional living quarters, perhaps for slaves. The area surrounding each single farmstead in the village was large. These compounds reflected the existence of a well-ordered society, with individual control of cattle and other resources.

Politically, Denmark was made up of petty rural kingdoms, as were its Scandinavian neighbours. The farmers and rulers were also warriors, and only in times of war did powerful kings emerge. One such king was Godfred, who defended the southern Danish frontier against Charlemagne shortly after 800. His troops erected a new frontier wall south of the market place of Hedeby (near present-day Schleswig), which was then refounded as a trading emporium. The extensive trade we have already discussed enriched the nobility from whom Godfred emerged, but for most people life went on much as usual.

In the ninth century there were only a couple of towns in Denmark, situated at the southern border and on the northern sea. These 'towns' were not provincial centres but market places of a very specialised nature geared to international trade. Significantly, men made up by far the largest part of the population (to judge by the size of the many shoes found and the skeletons in the burial yards). Hedeby, the best-known of these towns, was connected with Birka, in Sweden; Birka was connected with trading centres in Russia, and so on.[10]

Archaeology gives us a very clear idea of Hedeby. In the harbour area all land was registered. Between the plank-covered streets and lanes lay narrow plots on which stood lightly built wooden structures of one storey. The houses, which consisted of a main room and a couple of smaller workshops or storerooms, were constantly renewed. There was only a little free space around the buildings. The occupants of each dwelling changed at fairly short intervals, and there was no special quarter for any of the trades. The picture is very different to that of the later permanent towns which had much more room for both houses and communal activities.

Religion in Denmark, as in the rest of Scandinavia, centred round a number of gods whose behaviour probably resembled an idealised version of the life of the magnates; feasting, travelling, fighting and seeking excitement. In addition, the Vikings believed in lesser, often evil, supernatural beings, resembling the commoners. Also venerated were the forces of nature. As in Islam, the death of a warrior could mean a direct passage to Valhalla, the hall of the slain, in Asgard, the home of the gods. But in the stories the Vikings told about their gods there is a feeling of aimlessness, that all this activity had no deeper aims. Do we detect the same ideology in the arts of the Viking aristocracy, highly abstract and ornamental but almost completely lacking in content? This is perhaps the reason why the Vikings were absorbed so easily into the western European cultures of countries such as England and Scotland where they settled.[11]

51. Ornate cup from Jelling

In the second Viking Age, 950-1050, a new type of society emerged in Denmark; it became a centralised state with taxation of various kinds, strong kings and large armies. There were two main reasons for this. First, the system of agriculture – the cultivation of food on which all classes in society depended – underwent long-term changes. Second, there was northward pressure from a vigorous, expanding Germany which threatened the independence of the Danish lords. This external threat stimulated one royal family, the Jelling dynasty in Jutland (the area nearest to both Germany and England), to strengthen and broaden its political power, and to extend its defences.

The economic basis for this new kind of state lay in the developments that had taken place in agriculture. The leading echelons of Danish society showed a strong interest in cereal cultivation in the second Viking Age, whereas in the earlier days pastoral herding had been the dominant kind of farming. For example, at one of the royal fortresses, archaeologists have found a huge cache of rye seed-corn. The grains of this corn are unusually large, indicating that it came from either southeast Poland or the Ukraine, and demonstrating that even royal households were dependent on imported foodstuffs. With the increase in the cultivation of cereal crops came newer and sturdier types of plough, and the harrow was also probably introduced at about this time. People began to settle in stable agricultural communities where they held their land as private property and established a pattern of settlement that has lasted until the present day.

We also see the establishment of a new type of farm in Denmark, the magnate farm, or manor. One such magnate farm was found at Vorbasse in central Jutland.[12] The enclosure measures 120 x 215 metres, or more than two and a half hectares. In the middle of the manor was a splendid hall rivalled only by those of the royal fortresses. The hall was the living quarters of the landlord. At the periphery of the enclosure were stables with room for about one hundred large animals (cattle and horses), storerooms, servants' quarters and workshops. Several such magnate farms lie close together, overshadowing the property of the ordinary farmers. On these farms were also found water-mills for grinding cereals, a most important advance. Such farmsteads demonstrate how, in the late Viking Age, wealth in land was amassed on a scale not experienced before. This was the economic basis for the strong aristocracy and the powerful rulers, such as Canute, the Danish and English king, who dominated this era.

This fundamental change in agricultural practice meant that Denmark could feed and accommodate a very large population. Consequently, there was no need for a serious attempt to expand foreign settlements in the second Viking Age. The increased manpower, the new types of agriculture and settlement became the foundations for the state of Denmark, united under one king.

The Danish state was founded in Jutland. In about 960, at the royal centre of Jelling, King Harald erected a huge stone in memory of his parents and to emphasise his own newly-acquired power. The stone carries the image of Christ and a large animal fighting a snake, a masterpiece of Viking decorative art. The monument was placed next to Harald's great wooden church and between the two largest burial mounds in Denmark. One of these mounds probably held the bodies of Harald's parents, mentioned in the runic inscription on the stone:

> King Harald bade be made this monument after Gorm his father and Thyra his mother – that Harald who won for himself Denmark all, and Norway, and made the Danes Christian.

Harald accepted Christianity as the state religion (the earliest

52. The Jelling Stone

53. Jelling

54. The Trelleborg Fortress

representation of Christ in Scandinavia is on one side of the stone), a move calculated to identify his state with the western European countries and also to keep the German emperor at bay. A few years earlier the emperor had nominated German bishops to convert the pagan Danes, and had moved to seize Denmark as an imperial fief. With Denmark, or at least Jutland, officially Christian, the emperor lost any such pretext for trying to establish a foothold on Danish soil.

The core of King Harald's realm in Denmark was secured with fortifications. To the south, the ancient border walls were reinforced, to the north and east King Harald 'bade be made' magnificent circular fortresses of the Trelleborg type, modelled on a symmetrical plan and housing only large halls.[13] The largest of these fortresses was more than two hundred and fifty metres across and contained forty-eight identical wooden halls, each thirty-two metres long, arranged in blocks of four within a grid system of streets, three running north-south and three east-west. The earthen wall and the streets were covered with planks. Even the smallest of these fortresses (with only sixteen halls) required for its construction an enormous amount of wood, labour and provisions. Resources on this scale could only be marshalled by a very powerful and secure king.

In the centre of the state, the core area, we find the earliest provincial towns, regularly spaced throughout the countryside. These towns were very small by present-day standards but they were crucial to the functioning of the new economy. They acted as markets for produce from the surrounding areas, and as centres for craft manufacture for local consumption. Towns also contained the most important church institutions and housed royal representatives whose function was two-fold: to collect taxes and to supervise the collective life of the town. In some towns they also supervised the mint. The archaeological picture of these towns is still meagre, but massive deposits have been found, indicating continuity in settlement and a high measure of activity, not to mention lack of refuse collection. The lay-out of the towns was more open than in the harbour area of Hedeby in the ninth century. There was sufficient space for yards, and even stables. Wood was still the main building material, and remained so almost until modern times, but shortly after the year 1000 the first stone churches were constructed with the aid of English stonemasons.

The development of Denmark in the second Viking Age was undoubtedly costly for the state. The military sector alone, including ships, fortifications, the fortresses and so on, would easily have eaten up the traditional royal revenues. But in addition the state built up its infrastructure by improving roads and building bridges. To the south of the royal capital of Jelling, for example, a two-lane wooden bridge, almost a kilometre long, was constructed in King Harald's later years.

In order to pay for all this the king of Denmark started to look for new sources of income. The process began by extending control over eastern Denmark, which by the year 1000 was integrated into the kingdom, and mapped out with towns, markets and bishoprics. Norway and Sweden seem to have been much less developed in this period, and this prompted a rivalry between the Scandinavian nations that formed the background to a new wave of Scandinavian attacks on England in the second Viking Age.

In the 980s, Scandinavian pirates, at first Norwegians, returned to the coasts of England for booty. In 994, the Danish king, Sven, son of King Harald, led a direct assault on England. Already, in 991, the Vikings had extracted for the first time tribute payment in return for a promise of peace and safety, leaving with ten thousand pounds of silver. This impressive sum was, however, only a fraction of the total payments to the Danes in this period. By the year 1018, the English had paid almost two hundred and fifty thousand pounds of silver to the Danes, in ever increasing amounts. It is no wonder that Sven, and later his son Canute, were elected English kings. It was much cheaper to pay them ordinary tax than to continue to pay tribute.

In comparison, the French payments to the Vikings in the ninth century only amounted to about one sixth of the later English payments.[14] There is also another important difference. The money from the raids of the first Viking Age was spent abroad, while the money from England was fed back directly into the Danish economy. This income was exploited by Sven and Canute, and resulted in a doubling of the silver stock in Denmark. The other Scandinavian countries also benefited as the Danish kings bought the loyalty and support of a large number of Scandinavian leaders with the promise of booty from the assaults on England.

King Canute and his son managed to rule a North-Sea empire centred on England and Denmark, but only, and with interruptions, until 1042, when the English freed themselves from Danish rule, and the empire collapsed. In reality it was never possible for the Danes to administer both England and Denmark across wide stretches of sea, and in fact Canute was more a king of England than of Denmark. Such rule was based on military power and was motivated by easy gain. After the conquest it was no longer possible to extort tribute; it seems that the Danes had no plans for a continued political presence in England and may well have overreached themselves. For instance, after the conquest they dissolved most of the army and lost a crucial instrument of power.

Although the Danes were driven out for good in 1042, they did not lose interest in England and there were repeated attempts to reassert Scandinavian rule. The most famous attempt took place in 1066, when the Norwegian King Harald, an ex-mercenary officer at the court of the Byzantine emperor, was defeated at Stamford Bridge. Ironically, this was a few days before the Norman Conquest, staged by descendants of the Normandy Vikings, which was to establish a new and lasting order in England.

The collapse of its empire inevitably had repercussions in Denmark itself. Deprived of a major source of wealth in England, the Danes could no longer buy the support of their allies, and so were rendered vulnerable to attack. By this time the country must have looked much the same as England, although less developed: a rather prosperous, well-organised state, based on cereal agriculture and with towns and markets to help regulate the economy. In the cities there were bishops who maintained relations abroad, but the large-scale international trade was gone. Contacts with Germany and trade in the Baltic were, after all, more important than travelling across the North Sea to England, or to the Islamic East. Denmark had turned into a small and vulnerable west European state, raided by its barbarian neighbours.

The Viking Age does not constitute a unique stage in the development of European society. The Vikings were only active participants in a general process. However, they left an important legacy across Europe. The English language, for instance, has a very strong Danish component. You cannot *thrive*, or be *ill*, or *die* without speaking 'Danish'. Many place-names in England, and with the expansion of the English, all over the world, are therefore Scandinavian. No doubt elements of Viking organisation also survived in later English society. Viking technology, especially that relating to ships and navigation, was also very important, and even the characteristic Scandinavian art-forms survived into later periods, a reminder of the high status of the Viking leaders.

The two Viking Ages of expansion cannot simply be explained as a passive reaction to economic and political events. The Vikings seized the opportunities offered by these events to make Scandinavia one of the most dynamic societies at this time, and thus to influence the entire development of western Europe.

## Further reading

P.G. Foote and D.M. Wilson, *The Viking Achievement: The Society and Culture of Early Scandinavia* (London, 1970); J. Graham-Campbell and D. Kidd, *The Vikings* (London, 1980); R. Hodges, *Dark Age Economics: The Origins of Towns and Trade* AD*600-1000* (London, 1982); M. Lombard, *The Golden Age of Islam, North-Holland Medieval Translations*, vol. 2 (Amsterdam, Oxford and New York, 1975); K. Randsborg, *The Viking Age in Denmark: The Formation of a State* (London and New York, 1980); P.H. Sawyer, *Kings and Vikings: Scandinavia and Europe* AD*700-1100* (London and New York, 1982).

55. Viking raiders

CHAPTER EIGHT

# The Vikings in Britain

## Alfred P. Smyth

By AD800 the political map of Britain had taken on a recognisable shape. The Anglo-Saxons had consolidated their hold on lands from the Firth of Forth and from Galloway in the north, to Dover and Exeter in the far south. Not only had the four Anglo-Saxon kingdoms into which the country was now divided been Christian for two centuries, but the English had embraced Christianity with enthusiasm and a magnificent Christian civilisation had come into being, especially in Northumbria in the age of Bede. Here, 'north of Humber' (as the region was called), at centres such as York, Lindisfarne, Whitby and Jarrow, men and women lived in religious communities which housed some of the most gifted scholars and craftsmen in western Christendom. Further north, the Scots in Argyll had not yet conquered the whole of what we now call Scotland, but they had succeeded in evangelising the Picts in the north and east of the country. The Scottish church on Iona had become not only the centre of Scottish Christianity but a major cultural centre whose influence was felt as far afield as the court of the new Frankish empire.

Many of these important centres of sanctity and learning throughout Britain, such as Lindisfarne, Jarrow and Iona, were sited in exposed coastal areas. While these sanctuaries were safe from the turbulent Christian warriors in Dark Age Britain, they were vulnerable to attack from heathen neighbours from overseas. Suddenly and without warning, ferocious invaders from Northern Europe descended on Britain, and not only destroyed much of the outstanding cultural achievement resulting from years of Christian piety, but also altered the whole course of British history.

These invaders called themselves Vikingar – Vikings – and they came first from the fjords of Norway in search of land in the Scottish isles and loot from the monasteries of northern England. The *Anglo-*

*Saxon Chronicle* records the first 'ravages of [heathen men] who miserably destroyed God's church on Lindisfarne with plunder and slaughter' in June 793. The account of an earlier Viking raid on Dorset in *c*.789 is not (as it now stands) a contemporary record. Raids on Britain and Ireland increased in intensity over the next half century with scarcely a single monastery escaping the piratical greed of the invaders, until eventually a full-scale invasion was launched from Denmark in about 865 with a view to the outright conquest of the Anglo-Saxons.

This invading force, known to English observers as the 'Great Heathen Army', arrived off the coast of East Anglia in possibly as many as three or four hundred Viking longships in the autumn of 865. (The size of Viking fleets is still a matter of some dispute.)[1] The invasion was master-minded by the Danish king Ivar, known to Scandinavian legend as Ivar the Boneless and remembered by continental and British chroniclers as the most cruel of all Scandinavian sea-kings.

In Danish saga, Ivar was depicted as the all-conquering hero-king, borne aloft by his warriors on a shield as he led them into battle after battle all over western Europe. He was believed to have been the son of Ragnar Hairy Breeches, and Ivar was said to have invaded England to avenge the cruel death of his father Ragnar in a Northumbrian snake pit. The snake pit was a figment of the gruesome Norse

56. The Viking invasion of Britain

imagination, but Ivar and his brother Halfdan, commanders of that great Danish army, were all too real. They and their warriors swept across the eastern lowlands of England like a knife through butter.

In four years the invaders had toppled three of the four Anglo-Saxon kingdoms: Northumbria, Mercia and East Anglia. These Old English kingdoms and kings were to disappear forever, leaving Wessex holding out alone in the far south. By the 870s, Danish yeomen were settling down to plough some of the richest farmlands in England, from the Vale of York through the Lincolnshire wolds to the Thames estuary in Essex. In the far north-west, Norwegian warriors with their womenfolk were seizing the best farmland they could find along the coasts and on the Pennine slopes from the Solway to the Wirral. The northern and western isles and coasts of Scotland were also overrun by the invaders, and the Irish Sea turned into a Viking lake. Here the conquest of northern England in the 860s had been matched by the founding of Dublin in 841 as a major trading station from where Norsemen terrorised the population in the Irish hinterland. The 'Northmen' had come to Britain to stay.[2]

What were these Vikings really like and how can we account for their astonishing success? Romantics in the nineteenth century, in Wagner's Germany, in Victorian England, and obviously in Scandinavia itself, viewed the Norsemen as manly heroes – blameless freeborn warriors who symbolised all that was best in Germanic society and whose heroism foreshadowed the greatness of the British and German empires. A radical view which gained ground in the 1960s held that the Vikings were a rather misunderstood group who were judged harshly by the narrow-minded monks of medieval Christendom. They were seen as a bunch of well-meaning, long-haired tourists who now and then roughed up the natives in western Europe. However, traditional British and French scholars have sided with the monastic chroniclers in seeing the Norsemen as a barbarous scourge bent on the destruction of western civilisation.[3]

We can dismiss any illusions we may have inherited from our Victorian ancestors about Norse valour. The Scandinavian image of the swashbuckling hero defying death and seeking immortal glory on the battlefield simply does not bear close scrutiny. No advantage was too slight for the Vikings to exploit, and they consistently and – from their point of view – sensibly followed a strategy which brought them victory at the lowest possible cost in Norse lives. Vikings rarely fought pitched battles on open ground; they preferred to lure their enemies into an ambush, or to catch them unarmed and unawares. Thus York was captured on 1 November, the feast of All Saints, when the Northumbrians were trapped, unarmed and unprepared, celebrating a great Christian festival. Armagh in Ireland was regularly sacked on the feasts of its patrons, St Patrick (17 March) and St Martin (11 November), while St Martin's own monastery at Tours on the Loire was also sacked by Vikings on its founder's feast day. King Alfred once narrowly escaped death when King Guthrum's Danish army surprised him as he celebrated Twelfth Night, with few warriors in his household, on an isolated farm at Chippenham in north Wiltshire. Elsewhere, monks were butchered on Christmas night, frozen lakes were crossed to attack island sanctuaries, and endless records survive of defenceless fugitives being burnt alive when they had taken refuge in monastic buildings.[4] The twelfth century Icelanders remembered their Viking ancestors as past masters at surrounding their enemies' homes and burning unwary victims – men, women and children – in their beds, and Icelandic sagas, such as *Njal's Saga* or *Egil's Saga*, abound with such tales of Norse atrocities.[5] Much earlier and more reliable accounts than those in the sagas, from as far apart as the Hebrides and the Frankish empire, tell of monks being tortured to death to reveal the whereabouts of church treasure. An unfortunate monk, Blathmac, was torn limb from limb by Vikings on Iona in 825 because he refused to divulge the whereabouts of St Columba's shrine. Christian warlords in the Dark Ages were no saints, and were not averse to stealing from monasteries, but the catalogue of Norse atrocities from all over Western Europe seems endless and is consistently terrifying. There was a grotesque element in Norse barbarism which surpassed anything that had gone before.

These same ingredients which accounted for Viking success at local level – namely opportunism, surprise and terror – also lay behind their more spectacular conquests in France and England. True to style, the Norsemen only attacked countries which were either unprepared or in a state of disarray. They waited to invade the Frankish empire until Charlemagne's son, Louis the Pious, had died and the empire was being fought over by Louis' three sons. In Britain, too, the Vikings waited like vultures to seize their chance. The Danes waited more than half a century longer to launch their great invasion against England. They chose their time and their English victims carefully. Wessex in the south was the strongest kingdom; it was left alone until its weaker neighbours had been conquered. Although the Great Army landed in East Anglia, it singled out Northumbria for its initial onslaught; at the time a civil war was raging there with two rivals, Osbert and Ella and their opposing armies, fighting for control. The Vikings disposed of both rulers and soon overcame the kings of Mercia and East Anglia.

The Norsemen had mobility and surprise on their side, with longships providing swift access up rivers, and horses carrying warriors from the anchored fleets to targets further inland. Terror, too, was ever present, and the ghoulish rites of human sacrifice to the war-god Odin, kept a conquered English population suitably cowed. Norse accounts tell how Ivar the Boneless presided over the butchery of Ella, last of the Old English kings of Northumbria. The victim was made to look like a bloody spread-eagle, the favourite bird of Odin:

> Ivar caused the blood-eagle to be carved on the back of King Ella, and they cut away all of the ribs from his spine and then they ripped out his lungs.[6]

Next it was the turn of Edmund, last of the English kings of East Anglia, to be offered as a victim to the Germanic war-god. A Frankish monk, Abbo of Fleury, who knew nothing of Norse rituals and who wrote a century after Edmund's death at the hands of the same Ivar, tells us that after his capture in battle against the Danes:

> Saint Edmund's ribs were laid bare by numberless gashes, as if he had been tortured on the rack, or had been torn apart by savage claws.[7]

Not a pleasant fate, and it is little wonder that Edmund was soon revered as a saint.

Edmund was slain in November 869 and by then Ethelred, king of the West Saxons, alone survived as the last representative of Old English monarchy. The Norsemen launched their attack on Wessex at Reading in the spring of 870. Ethelred died in the midst of this crisis and was succeeded by his younger brother Alfred, who became king of the West Saxons soon after Easter 871. To make matters worse, a great new army of Danes arrived at Reading to reinforce the invaders who were already in control of the town.

Alfred's defence of his beleaguered kingdom has caught the imagination of generations of English men and women, and for obvious reasons this was one of the most critical periods of English history. If Alfred had lost, England would have undoubtedly become a Scandinavian land and might well have remained so to this day. By saving Wessex, Alfred saved England, in the sense that he provided a breathing space for English culture to sink ever deeper roots into the soil of Britain; these were roots which proved capable of withstanding future Danish conquest under Canute and even, in many respects, the conquest by William of Normandy. Of course, Alfred did not save England from invasion and military conquest in the longer term, nor could he stem the Scandinavian influence which was flooding into England outside Wessex in his own time.

It is very difficult to build up an accurate picture of this king's reign since he was an expert propagandist and kept tight control over how the history of the Danish wars was recorded. Alfred's success can be put down to the king's own intelligence and to no small amount of luck, rather than to his ability as a warrior. Contrary to popular opinion, he was not a very successful warrior-king. His son Edward, and grandson Athelstan, far outclassed him in battle. Indeed, of the first five battles Alfred fought against the invaders he won only one, and it was the chance departure of the Danes from his kingdom in 872 (to put down a Northumbrian revolt) that gave him a much needed breathing space. Even during this period of truce he was forced to pay the invaders tribute, and on their return to the fray four years later he continued to lose ground rapidly, retreating to the western fringes of his kingdom.

All seemed lost when in 878 the Danish king, Guthrum, almost captured Alfred on his country estate at Chippenham in the depths of winter. Alfred escaped with his royal household and withdrew even further west into the Somerset marshes. He was intelligent enough to realise that reckless heroics would get him nowhere against the Danes and the time had come to beat them at their own game. He built a fortress at Athelney in the Somerset marshes; from there he proceeded to terrorise the countryside which had recently been settled by the Danish invaders. Meanwhile, the Great Army of the Danes had been whittled away. It was fifteen years since the invaders had arrived and most had by now settled down to till the soil across the length and breadth of northern and eastern England. Alfred had reversed roles with his enemies – he was now at the head of a warband that was constantly on the move, and the Danes were trying to protect their land. Alfred rapidly wore down the opposition and showed the faint-hearted English in Wessex and Kent that he was still their king and capable of resisting the oppressor. By May 878 he felt strong enough to take on Guthrum and his warriors in pitched battle. Alfred rode out to a place called Egbert's Stone, east of Selwood, where the men of Somerset, Wiltshire and Hampshire rallied to his banner. Two days later at Edington he fought and won that amazing victory which turned the reign of a fugitive king into a long-remembered triumph. Not only were the Danes defeated and forced to withdraw from Wessex, but Guthrum and thirty of his chief warriors were forced to accept Christian baptism.

We must be careful not to overestimate Alfred's military victory at Edington or to underestimate the effect of Guthrum's baptism. Guthrum was still strong enough to treat Alfred as an equal, and he withdrew honourably to East Anglia where he ruled until his death. But by accepting Christianity, Guthrum was turning his back on the dark and bloodthirsty rites of the Germanic war-god and paying lip-service at least to the more civilised rules of Christian life. The Danish

57. Silver penny of St Edmund

leader took the English royal name of Athelstan at his baptism; soon his followers in East Anglia were being evangelised by English priests and teachers and inevitably began to absorb the English way of life. Within a few years of the brutal murder of Edmund by Ivar the Boneless, silver pennies commemorating St Edmund's martyrdom were circulating among the newly converted Danes of East Anglia.

Further north at York, where Danish rule was strongest and survived longest, the conquerors were just as quickly influenced by English life and customs. In York and Northumbria, the Danes were faced with a local population they could neither annihilate nor outnumber and some sort of agreement had to be reached. Since the church was the most powerful English organisation which had survived the fall of the Old English monarchy, the Vikings had no choice but to do business with it. This alliance between northern English Christians and the Danish invaders was not always understood by patriotic chroniclers in Wessex; they could not comprehend, for example, how the Archbishop of York could have given Christian

58. Viking tombs from York Minster

59. Stone depicting a snake pit

burial to 'the hateful Danish king' Guthfrith in 895, in the hallowed setting of York Minster alongside tombs of the ancient kings of Northumbria.

Excavations in York Minster have uncovered Viking tombs in the vicinity of the Anglo-Saxon cathedral, showing how the church was willing to confer respectability on the heathen Dane provided the invader was prepared to safeguard religious liberties. Quite remarkably, one of these stones even shows a man dying in a snake pit, a reminder of the Danish legend that Ivar the Boneless conquered Northumbria to avenge his father's death in just such a pit. From this time, too, we find the York clergy at liberty to issue a splendid series of silver pennies from York Minster and, even more astonishing, that same clergy helped to design and mint a series of coins for the new Danish kings.[8] Illiterate Viking rulers, such as Canute, who issued their silver pennies in about the year 900, were in no position to read even their own names on these coins, but they were no doubt eager to ape the English king in Wessex and continental Christian rulers, in having a coinage in their newly conquered kingdoms. Coinage, like writing and Christianity, was a novelty for the Vikings, but it was also essential if the Danish colony in Britain were to survive. The killing and looting could not go on forever. Besides, there were limits to monastic treasure, and the violence and brutality of the early days had to give way to more settled conditions of farming and trade if Norse women and their children were to be attracted from Scandinavia.

It is known that women came with the warriors from the beginning. The Anglo-Saxon chronicler speaks of them in south-east England as

60, 61, 62, 63. Silver pennies of Cnut, Guthrum, Gothfrithsson and Eric Bloodaxe

early as the 890s, and their bodies have been found in early pagan Viking cemeteries at York and Dublin, laid out in death with their Scandinavian brooches and adornments. These Scandinavian ladies established households in the towns and countryside of eastern and northern England. Such households needed peace to survive; very soon the aims of ordinary Norse men and women began to coincide more and more with those of the conquered English population, and to move further away from the heady world of beer-drinking warriors of an earlier generation.

We gain a vivid insight into the lives of the Danish colonists from studying the remains of their timber houses which survive crowded together in tenth century York. Excavations here and at the sister Viking town of Dublin have revealed a wealth of information on conditions in which Scandinavian traders and their families lived at this time.[9] Wattle and plank walls of houses have been uncovered standing to a height of more than a metre, with evidence also for the roofing and detailed layout of the interiors. These houses, which stood end-on to the street, were inhabited by the traders and craftsmen who built up Scandinavian York and Dublin into leading cities in the western Viking world. We find tanneries, and leather workshops, together with houses occupied by craftsmen who worked in metal and bone. It is the evidence for the scale of production which is most remarkable and leaves us with the decided impression that it was Viking industry and trade which revived urban life in the old decaying town centres of Britain which had died – commercially at least – after the withdrawal of the Roman legions over four hundred years earlier.[10]

As the burghers of York and Northumbria grew ever richer on international trade and as the Old English church in the north shared in this new-found security and wealth, a new political attitude developed towards Wessex which was now rapidly expanding northwards over the Midlands and towards the Humber. The kings of Wessex and their archbishop at Canterbury were pursuing a patriotic war against the Danish settlers, with a view to uniting England for the first time under a king of Wessex. However, to the Northumbrian English and their archbishop, Wulfstan, it was preferable to back the Danish kings of York and Dublin, rather than to submit to men of Wessex who never had any claims on York, even before the Danish wars began. Archbishop Wulfstan also had to consider the future of his own powerful position if he were not to be overshadowed by Wessex and the Archbishop of Canterbury. As for the king of the Scots, he also preferred to see a friendly Danish kingdom in northern England, to act as a buffer between him and the ambitious kings of Wessex. So a great alliance was formed between Olaf, king of York and Dublin, and Constantine II, king of Scots, in an effort to drive the men of Wessex out of northern England and back behind their own borders. Wessex was at this time ruled by Athelstan, grandson of Alfred the Great and he met the combined armies of York, Dublin and Scotland at a place called Brunanburh in 937.

It was here on this unidentified battlefield that the House of Alfred won its greatest military triumph, and here too, significantly, that the grandson of Alfred defeated Olaf, great-grandson of Ivar the Boneless, who had butchered Edmund of East Anglia nearly seventy years earlier. The *Anglo-Saxon Chronicle* leaves us in no doubt as to the outcome of this battle:

> In this year, King Athelstan lord of nobles, dispenser of treasure to men, and his brother also, Edmund Atheling, won by the sword's edge undying glory in battle round Brunanburh. Never yet in this island, by what books tell us and our ancient sages, was a greater

> slaughter of a host made by the edge of the sword, since the Angles and Saxons came hither from the east, invading Britain over the broad seas, [when they] overcame the Britons and won a country.[11]

Although Wessex won, there were heavy casualties on both sides, and both Constantine and Olaf survived to fight another day. Two years later Athelstan died and Olaf, ever ready to exploit a weak situation, returned to attack Athelstan's younger brother and successor, King Edmund. This time the situation was reversed. The heathen Olaf, with the help of the Archbishop of York, confronted the men of Wessex at Leicester and forced them to retreat behind a line from Chester to London, roughly along the route of the old Roman Watling Street. At Leicester in 940 Olaf Gothfrithsson took the York kingdom to the height of its power. York became the dominant kingdom in the British Isles controlling most of England and all of the Irish coastal towns, while exercising overlordship in the Scottish isles. But Olaf's achievement and his strong government were a very personal affair. He alone succeeded in uniting the far flung Danish and Norwegian strongholds in the British Isles. As Archbishop Wulfstan watched Olaf's successors lose more and more ground to Wessex, he began to cast around for new war leaders.

Eventually, Wulfstan and the Northumbrian 'royal council' invited the notorious Norwegian king, Eric Bloodaxe, to rule at York. Eric had recently been expelled from his throne in Norway for his tyrannical rule. He was welcomed in York with his queen Gunnhild in 948, and for the next six years he held on to his precarious throne in defiance of every neighbouring kingdom in Britain. Such an unstable situation could not last, and Eadred, the new king of Wessex, realising that Danish York now relied solely on the support of Archbishop Wulfstan and his clergy, succeeded in capturing Wulfstan, bringing him as a prisoner to Wessex. It was a bold move and it worked. Eric fled from York in 954 and headed north and west along the old Roman road to Carlisle. The party included Eric and his household bodyguards, four other Norse kings, and two sons of the Norse earl of Orkney. They were probably hoping to sail from the Solway to the Orkneys, but they were ambushed as they crossed the heights of Stainmore in the Pennines, and Eric and his attendant kings were all killed.

The fall of Eric Bloodaxe and his Danish kingdom left Eadred of Wessex undisputed ruler of a new united realm of England. Northern England had experienced almost a century of Scandinavian rule, which was to leave its mark not only on the place-names of the area and the street names of York, but also on the whole future of English life. The Viking invasions had turned northern and eastern England into an Anglo-Danish land, introducing a new class of merchants and urban craftsmen as well as free land-owning warriors whose way of life and language was to have a significant influence on English society. Scandinavian art-forms and social customs were to dominate English life in the tenth and eleventh centuries. In the longer term this Danish colony prepared the way for the conquest by William of Normandy. The Viking wars had rudely awakened Anglo-Saxon England out of its long and relatively peaceful slumber. A warning note had been sounded: England was to become a prize, fought over by the Scandinavian north and its powerful colony across the Channel in Normandy.

## Further reading

J. Graham-Campbell, *Viking Artefacts: a Select Catalogue* (London, 1980); H.R. Loyn, *The Vikings in Britain* (London, 1977); P.H. Sawyer, *Kings and Vikings: Scandinavia and Europe* AD*700-1100* (London, 1982); Alfred P. Smyth, *Scandinavian York and Dublin: the History and Archaeology of Two Related Viking Kingdoms*, 2 vols (Dublin and New Jersey, 1975 and 1979); D. Whitelock, *The Anglo-Saxon Chronicle (60BC-AD1042)* in *English Historical Documents c.500-1042*, gen. ed. D.C. Douglas (London, reprint, 1968), vol. I, pp. 135-235.

CHAPTER NINE

# One English Nation

## Pauline Stafford

Although technically the kingdom of England dates from 954, it is a date which looks significant only with hindsight. In the mid-tenth century, Eadred's victory would have appeared to be just one more of a series of triumphs and reverses for the kings of Wessex. Eadred, now the sole king of the English, did not create a unified kingdom even though he ruled from the Channel coasts to the Scottish lowlands, and from Offa's Dyke to the North Sea. No feeling of nationalism bound the people together. Elements of unity existed, especially in the church, and the basis for strong kingship was there. But these factors were still balanced by deep divisions and local loyalties. The problems of consolidating an English kingdom remained when the dust of victorious battles had settled.

A year after the submission of York, Eadred died, prematurely, in his mid-thirties. The confusion which followed laid bare the reality of the new kingdom. Within two years Eadred's nephews had divided England between them, the elder ruling Wessex and the region south of the Thames, his brother Edgar taking Mercia and Northumbria. Rivalry between brothers had given old loyalties the chance to re-assert themselves, just as these older loyalties had fostered Edgar's rebellion. The division ended with the sudden death of the elder brother, Eadwig, but prior to this a group of great churchmen, supporters of Edgar, had been working to make him king of all England. Such reforming churchmen were committed not to division but to unity; they turned a separatist movement for independence into a plan to place Edgar on the throne of England. In 958 Archbishop Oda had moved against Eadwig and forcibly divorced him from his wife. The tide was turning even before Eadwig's death in 959, allowing Edgar, king of Mercia and Northumbria, to become Edgar, king of the English.

64. 'One King under one God'

In 1016 Edgar's ill-fated son, Ethelred the Unready, lay dying in London. England had been overcome once more by Vikings. In 1013 Sven Forkbeard, king of Denmark, had sailed his fleet in triumph to Gainsborough on the Trent and there received the submission of the Northumbrians, of the men of Lindsey and of the Danish settlers of north-east Mercia. He had then moved south to drive Ethelred into

65. Silver penny showing Edgar as king

66. Document showing Edgar as king

exile. By 1016 Sven was dead and Ethelred returned. But Sven's son Canute had been hailed king of England by his own army, and Ethelred's own son Edmund was in rebellion against his father, supported by the Northumbrians and a group of nobles in north-east Mercia. The stress of fifteen years and more of external attack and defeat by Viking armies had opened up rifts in the fragile unity of England.

Ethelred's death resulted in further rivalry between Edmund and Canute, and once again Wessex separated from Mercia and Northumbria. But in 1016 the strengths of the new English kingdom were apparent. We can appreciate the length of resistance and the loyalty of so many nobles, remarkable at a date when successful kingship was still largely synonymous with military success. We can see the role of a town such as London, itself largely a product of the tenth century revival of towns and trade, which held out so strongly that Canute later punished its citizens with harsh taxation; and we can hear the voice of the Archbishop of York, preaching even in the depths of defeat a powerful call to belief in one God and loyalty to a single king of England.

Danish invasion and settlement during the late ninth and early tenth centuries had created a sizeable Danish population in northern and eastern England. In 1013 it was these Danish areas which first submitted to Sven, and when he marched south he restrained his ravaging until his army crossed Watling Street, the line which Alfred had drawn in the 880s as the boundary of Danish rule.[1]

It is easy but perhaps mistaken to see the Danish settlers as an obstacle to unification. They appear as a problem towards the end of Ethelred's reign; when England was under attack by a Danish king, Danes in England were inevitably suspect. One chronicler snidely records that the leaders of a retreating army in Lindsey in 993 were men of Danish ancestry.[2] By 1002, suspicion was running so high that the king ordered a massacre of the Danes in England, because he had been informed that they would treacherously deprive him of his life and possess his kingdom afterwards.[3] The call was obeyed, as at Oxford where the Danes were pursued into the sanctuary of a church which was then burnt, books, ornaments, Danes and all.[4] The massacre was probably aimed at traders rather than at the settled Anglo-Danish community, but it must have powerfully contributed to the atmosphere of suspicion. In times of crisis people look for easy scapegoats, and an ethnic minority such as the Danish community in the early eleventh century was an identifiable group. Branded as treacherous, some men of Danish descent probably acted accordingly.

The result was that in 1013 and 1015 England was divided in a new way, not along the Thames between Wessex and Mercia, but along Watling Street; it was not Mercia which submitted to Sven, but Danish Mercia. Suspicion and Danish attack had fostered an existing sense of identity, already kept alive by the fact that the Danes had their own laws and their own court, that of the Five Boroughs of Leicester, Lincoln, Stamford, Nottingham and Derby.[5] The visual art of north-east Mercia and Yorkshire in the tenth century, especially the ubiquitous stone sculpture, shows a cultural blend of Danish and English distinct from that of southern England.[6]

But the Danish settlements were not a permanent obstacle to unification. The 'problem of Danish England' if it existed at all, was acute largely in the early eleventh century, sharpened by the strains

67. The division of England on Watling Street

68. Stone Anglo-Scandinavian tombs

and stresses of Ethelred's reign. It must be weighed against the careers of Danish immigrants such as Archbishop Oda and his nephew Archbishop Oswald. This son and grandson of Danish settlers were fierce supporters of the southern kings and of unity; they were champions of the new reform movement centred on the royal court. Oswald's loyalty was considered so unswerving that he could be trusted with the archbishopric of York, the most sensitive church appointment in the tenth century. Sons of Danish settlers, with perhaps less local feeling, were not obvious barriers to the process of unity. So, when England split again in 1035, it was the older pattern of Mercia and Northumbria against Wessex which reasserted itself. Few people actually felt English in the late tenth century and the identity of Mercians, Northumbrians and West Saxons was arguably more important than that of Danes.

The kingdom had been the product of conquest and accident. When the Northumbrians submitted to Eadred in 954 they were bowing to a conqueror who had ravaged them, burnt down the venerable old minster at Ripon and had barely been restrained from destroying the land utterly.[7] A healthy sense of self-preservation, not national feeling, made the men of York turn from the Norwegian Eric to the southern king of Wessex. The politically conscious were as likely to think of themselves as Mercians or Northumbrians as English. Edgar might usually be described on his coins and in some charters as 'king of the English', and it is significant that he thought of himself in that way. Some of his subjects obviously did too, but an anonymous poet in 975 preferred to call him 'ruler of the Angles, friend of the West Saxons and protector of the Mercians', while to others his brother Eadwig had been 'king of the Angles, the Northumbrians, pagans and Britons'.[8] 'England' in the late tenth century still had much of the quality of a confederacy about it.

If the identity of Mercians, Northumbrians and West Saxons was a political fact of the late tenth century, it was one which was preserved and encouraged in the ways that the new kingdom was ruled. The king controlled England through officials called ealdormen: the local government alderman preserves the title but none of the reality of this office. Ealdormen were provincial governors ruling great tracts of England, holding courts, dispensing patronage, leading out armies. By the end of Edgar's reign they ruled over areas essentially the same as the old kingdoms of the eighth and ninth centuries: Aelfhere was ealdorman of the Mercians, Aethelwine of the East Angles, Beorhtnoth of the East Saxons. In name and boundary the identities of lost kingdoms were kept alive; an ealdorman was at one and the same time a royal official and a focus of local loyalty.

For the local nobility this was the man who led them out in battle,

69. The King with his ealdormen

heard their cases in court, granted them land in life and heard their last testament at the point of death. His power and patronage might be exercised in the king's name, but his local role was bound to bring his allegiances under pressure. The ealdormen were the products and beneficiaries of unification, enjoying the new opportunities for wealth and influence created by the new kingdom. The mid-century description of one of them as Athelstan Half-King was no exaggeration.[9] Together with a few churchmen, especially the Archbishop of York, they were the potential foci and galvanisers of separatist feeling, on occasion deciding the fate of kings, particularly during disputes over the throne. To tenth century kings and their advisers the political question was not so much the abstract one of how to unify England, but the concrete one of winning and keeping the loyalty of nobles and churchmen.

The formal unification which 954 marked thus left many problems unanswered. Some of these were to be exacerbated during the late tenth and eleventh centuries, by the strains of Danish attack in Ethelred's reign, which put all loyalty under stress, and by methods of rule which placed old kingdoms under powerful royal officials. At this date all princes still had claims on the throne; the eldest was coming to be preferred, but younger brothers could lay a legitimate claim and, if they attracted sufficient support, make it good. The last century of Anglo-Saxon England is marked by a series of bitter disputes over the succession,[10] fostered at least in part because princes knew they could find support among those unhappy with the politics of unification. Edgar in 957, Ethelred in 975, Edmund in 1015 all based rebellion on dissident groups of nobles in Mercia, Northumbria and the Danelaw. Princely ambition utilised separatist feeling, and in the process reminded men of their local identity. But that same desire for power led most princes to harness local support not for a division of the kingdom, but in a bid to gain the throne of a unified England. If their actions fostered separatism they also demonstrate that for many men a unified England had advantages. Balancing the problems left by 954 were those developments already pulling against separatism, moving towards a consolidated kingdom of England.

Administrative change was one of these factors, although there were certainly no simple legislative answers to the problems. The map of English shires, as they existed until the Local Government Act of 1974, was largely drawn in the tenth century. Those of Wessex were there already; Devon, Cornwall, Sussex and Kent belong to the earlier history of England south of the Thames. East Anglia was an old kingdom: its division into the Northfolk and the Southfolk (Norfolk and Suffolk) is pre-tenth century. But the shires of Mercia were new creations. All take their name from a central town: *Leicester*shire, *Warwick*shire, *Nottingham*shire, *Gloucester*shire and so on. They centre on a borough which in the tenth century meant a fortified place. Their creation had much to do with defence and its maintenance. Their boundaries follow natural geography, but also reflect the political realities of their time. The Trent, for example, is the boundary between Nottinghamshire and Lincolnshire, but it is Watling Street, the boundary of Danish and English Mercia which separates Leicestershire and Warwickshire.

North of the Tees and west of the Pennines the authority of the English kings was thin; their shire system was not imposed here. Yorkshire, the effective frontier of their power, was the most northerly shire created before the Norman Conquest. Its boundaries go back to seventh century Deira; their retention by tenth century kings is one more reminder of the realities of their rule, of their anxiety to maintain a large defensive unit in the north, and even more of their reluctance to alienate local feeling there. Within these shires were administrative subdivisions, known as hundreds in southern England and English Mercia, and wapentakes in the areas north and east of Watling Street.

Shires, hundreds and wapentakes were meeting places of local communities. The new kings of England rearranged boundaries, defined the functions of the courts and regularised their meetings under royal control. Hundreds and wapentakes were to meet every four weeks 'and each man is to do justice to another'; shires were to meet half yearly.[11] The king appointed the presidents who sat in all the courts. Royal responsibility showed kings providing 'good rule and lordship' that nebulous concept which lay at the heart of successful political relations in the tenth century. Control ensured the king's share of the fines taken in court, and all late Saxon kings had a sharp eye for money. But, equally important, it was in the shire court that the great nobles of the tenth century met. When a royal messenger such as Abbot Aelfhere brought the seal of King Ethelred to Cuckamsley, in Berkshire, with the request that the case of Wynflaed be settled, he brought also a reminder of royal power;[12] when a writ was read out to the shire court, such as the one bringing Canute's friendly greetings to the assembled nobles and churchmen of Kent, it informed them of his gifts to Archbishop Aethelnoth and told them simultaneously of the advantages of royal patronage. In the courts of hundred and shire, royal authority came into direct contact with loyal communities and the delicate business of building loyalty began.

Administrative solutions depended entirely on the loyalty of the local nobility for their success; if the system did not work beyond the Tees and the Pennines it was partly because that loyalty was not forthcoming here. It could be secured by force, the ultimate sanction of royal power. When Eadred attacked the rebellious north in the 940s he took the Archbishop of York prisoner; in 952 he wreaked vengeance on the borough of Thetford and waged punitive campaigns in Northumbria two years later. Ethelred murdered or exiled numerous noblemen and in 1016 ravaged the old kingdom of Lindsey for its complicity in the Danish invasions. Late Anglo-Saxon rule was still based on the military prestige of the dynasty, and backed by the threat of exile or murder. But the use of force, while an effective means of subduing the kingdom in the short run, could not by itself guarantee permanent stability. Ravaging is not ruling, and resort to exile or murder is less a mode of political action than a sign that the political process itself has broken down.

To secure loyalty the king must be a 'good lord' and that still primarily meant a good giver, of land, money, office or women. Grants of land were made, especially to royal officials and churchmen. In a crisis, royal largesse mushroomed; when Eadwig was uncertain of his throne in 956 he made more grants of land in a single year than in many other entire reigns. Men were wooed or bound through marriage, women having always been the most important gift exchanged between men. And when Ethelred's father, Edgar, appointed Ordgar ealdorman of south-west England he married Ordgar's daughter; later stories of the king's seduction can be set aside, for marriage bound families together and the woman became almost a hostage at the royal court.[13] During the critical last years of his reign Ethelred married three of his daughters to the key ealdormen who controlled his defences.[14] But a king cannot marry the daughter of every noble, even though divorce and remarriage were still relatively easy in the tenth century. Offices were limited in number, land never plentiful enough to satisfy all demands. And in any case the king had little to give to northern nobles. Even his physical presence was rare north of the Trent. If loyalty was to be bought a regular cash income was a more secure and flexible basis.

Tenth century England was wealthy. Land changed hands rapidly in a burgeoning market, and its new owners, whether monastic houses, royal officials or minor nobility, were exploiting it more efficiently and more vigorously. The result was an upswing of local demand which combined with rapidly developing trade to stimulate town growth. By the 990s a high quality silver coinage circulated in millions. As many as forty million coins may have been struck in one six-year period alone and that at a time when a sheep was worth three pence and enough whey to feed a female slave for the summer could be had for a penny.[15] This was the wealth that was tapped and turned to political use by kings. From the end of Ethelred's reign there was a land tax to pay mercenaries, one of the earliest examples of direct taxation in Europe. Cash came also from royal lands, from the towns and from control of the coinage. In 973 Edgar finally established royal control of the system and of the profits from the striking of coins.[16] In a growing economy it was a stroke of genius. As the coinage swelled in response to rising trade royal income swelled with it, securing a renewable source of wealth to buy followers and maintain royal splendour. This source of wealth was also coveted by the Danish kings, and paid out in the Danegelds of Ethelred's reign (forty-eight thousand pounds of silver in 1012 alone).[17]

The tenth century trade revival stimulated town growth and the rising importance of the merchant group. The citizens of Danelaw towns such as York or Lincoln imported wine, Scandinavian walrus ivory and amber and lava quernstones, and manufactured trinkets for wives and girlfriends.[18] Stamford mass-produced cheap pottery bowls for local sale and expensive glazed ware for export.[19] Trade had always been under royal protection. It required safe movement, a coinage which could be trusted, protected weights and measures and regulated town courts to solve disputes. These safeguards for a vulnerable and often mobile mercantile group could only be guaranteed by strong kingship. The traders of tenth century England transcended old boundaries and became an added force for unity. The Londoners were loyal to Ethelred to the last, and in 954, in the debates which must have preceded Eric's expulsion from Northumbria, it is not hard to imagine the arguments deployed by those York merchants who already traded with southern England.

Another group committed to unity had been created within the upper ranks of the nobility by developments which unification itself had put in train. Ealdormen might be tempted to identify with local loyalties, but they also had wider landed interests which broadened their perspective. Many of them had been chosen originally from among the West Saxon nobility, and they retained land and family connections south of the Thames even after appointment to East Anglia or Mercia.[20] In the late tenth century York was ruled by men with estates in the southern Danelaw or Mercia.[21] Royal grants to these men deliberately reinforced this pattern of widely scattered estates. A close identity of interest was built up between an English king and a group of nobles whose landed possessions increasingly marked them as an English rather than a Mercian or Northumbrian nobility. This identity found expression in the patronage given by this group to the monastic revival, a court-centred religious movement with important political implications.

If unity was a question of loyalties, loyalty was more than a simple commodity to be bought. It was also an ideal to be wooed. 'Let us all love and honour one God, and zealously hold one Christian faith and entirely cast off every heathen practice . . . under the rule of one king'.[22] Archbishop Wulfstan II of York wrote these words in a lawcode of Ethelred in 1008. They echoed the sentiments of churchmen of his generation. Such men had the clearest idea of unity. They wished to create on earth a reflection of that order and unity which they felt characterised the kingdom of heaven, an aim to be achieved under the direction of wise strong kings. For them, as for traders, such kings were a practical necessity. Christianity was still so poorly established that there was need for legislation against those who worshipped fire or flood, wells, stones and forest trees; legislation was also needed to stop priests saying mass in unconsecrated buildings without altar wine.[23] In such a society, as in the age of the conversion, the close co-operation of reforming churchmen and king was still mutually necessary.

But strong kings and unity were also an ideal, a parallel of the heavenly kingdom and the rule of God. Reforming churchmen backed royal power with an ideology which compared kings to Christ and Christ to kings, and expressed it in stone and ink. 'For the king is Christ's deputy in a Christian people. . . .' Such ideas were preached to the nobility, written into the laws read out in the shire courts, and reiterated daily in the monasteries which now sprang up throughout southern England. Men raised in these traditions made loyal abbots and bishops, and were appointed to sees as far north as York and Durham, areas where royal influence was thin.[24] Churchmen mattered politically at a date when they still led out armies and sat in judgement in the shire courts, and when the church held as much as a fifth of all

70. Edgar flanked by his archbishops

the land in England.

On Whit Sunday 973 Edgar was crowned and anointed Emperor of Britain; the ceremony took place in Bath, chosen for its physical reminders of Roman imperial might. A contemporary observer described how the king arrived with a crowd of abbots, abbesses and priests.[25] Two bishops took him by the hand and led him into the church where the great nobles were already assembled. There Dunstan and Oswald anointed him to the sound of the antiphon 'Sadoc the priest and Nathan the prophet anointed Solomon king'; then the cry was raised 'May the king live for ever'. At the banquet afterwards the king, seated between the archbishops, was surrounded by ealdormen, royal officials, great nobles – 'all the dignity of the English'. Edgar went on to issue a new lawcode, to publish his reform of the coinage and then to sail with his fleet to Chester. There the Welsh princes met him and in a ritual gesture of submission rowed him along the River Dee; the princes manned the oars, while Edgar held the rudder. The whole series of events was political theatre: Edgar the Emperor of Britain, a military ruler, the Lord's anointed. It was image creation as much as reality, but nevertheless a powerful image.

In the early eleventh century, England was ruled by foreigners; first the Danish Canute and his sons, his Norman queen Emma and by 1042 by Edward the Confessor, the half-French, half-English son of Emma and Ethelred. The lack of immediate problems underlines the absence of strong national feeling as we understand it. Strong kingship mattered as much as the individual dynasty, unity more than Englishness.[26] The frequent absence of Danish kings *did* strain an essentially personal system of government and aided the rise of noble families arguably even more powerful than before. Old divisions were still apparent and the redistribution of royal patronage to foreigners upset the old patterns of noble expectations and the delicate web of king/noble relations. But ominous new grievances were appearing directed against strong kingship itself.[27] When the men of Worcester murdered King Harthacnut's tax collectors in 1041 they expressed resentment at royal exactions, fanned and legitimized by the fact of a Danish king. The very success of the processes of unification was already altering the nature of the political issues.

In 1042 Edward the Confessor's inheritance was a united England. His ancestors may have offered what often seem fragile and short-term answers to deep-seated problems, but they had held together a kingdom for a century. In so doing they had sufficiently weakened existing divisions and loyalties, and created or played upon forces for unity, that by the mid-eleventh century the prize for which princes and conquerors fought was the entire kingdom of England itself.

## Further reading

J. Campbell (ed.), *The Anglo-Saxons* (Oxford, 1982); M. Dolley, *Anglo-Saxon Coins* (London, 1983); R.A. Hall (ed.), *Viking Age York and the North* (London, 1978); D. Hill (ed.), *Ethelred the Unready*, British Archaeological Reports, British Series, 59 (Oxford, 1978); P.A. Stafford, *The East Midlands in the Early Middle Ages* (Leicester, 1984).

71. The peoples of Scotland

CHAPTER TEN

# The Kingdom of the Scots

A.A.M. Duncan

Scotland is a hybrid word whose first syllable is of unknown derivation but comes to us from speakers of a Celtic tongue, and whose second syllable is an English word. The very name is a good summation of the earliest history of an emergent Celtic kingdom which extended itself to control an English province, and changed from a scatter of provinces, held together uncertainly by the most masterful of the provincial kings, to a kingdom whose unchallenged ruler was supported by resources in both men and money. It is not an easy story to tell because our sources are so few, so brief, and so distant, for they were all written in Ireland or England.[1]

The most decisive but not necessarily the best informed of the early sources is Bede, who wrote in about 730 of the warlike Picts. They lived in most of the land north of the Forth and were Christianised from Iona, the great monastery of St Columba, by the Scots, whose lands were separated from those of the Picts by the mountain range known as Druimalban. Those Picts have left traces in the place-names of their language, which belongs to the same Celtic family as Welsh. These include the *Aber* names of Scotland. *Aber* means the confluence or mouth of a river as in Aberdeen – mouth of the Dee – or Aberlemno. But the place-name element most commonly used to illustrate the Picts is Pit (as in Pitlochry), whose meaning is explained by the cognate English words 'bit' and 'piece'. The pit names are found just where Bede implies the Picts lived.[2]

The second relic of this enigmatic people is the vivid carving of the so-called symbol stones, a striking group of which is to be found at Aberlemno. The symbols themselves are a cause of unending debate, for they occur in no obvious pattern of combinations, and it is far from certain that the stones are funerary monuments, for even those found in kirkyards may have been moved there by later, more pious

72. The Aberlemno Kirkyard Stone

generations.[3] However, the accompanying scenes of hunting or great battles are surely the equivalent of the heroic poetry of the Anglo-Saxons, the Pictish record of the same aristocratic pursuits of hunting, fighting to the death in loyalty to a lord, and hard drinking. And on the other side, we find the other side of life, a different claim, the cross of Christ.

It is unlikely that the ethos and life-style of the Scots in Argyll was significantly different, even if they were producing sculpture that seems more conventional to our eyes because it is wholly Christian. Nevertheless, the distinction between Scots and Picts is a real one because the former spoke Irish, a Celtic language of a different group from Welsh or Pictish. It also seems real because we know the names of two lines of kings, those of the Scots and those of the Picts, and this conjures up a simple picture of two kingdoms corresponding to two peoples.[4] Almost certainly those two kinglists were a gross over-simplification of political reality, for the Picts inhabited districts with distinct names which had their own rulers whom the Irish would call by their word for king. What the Picts called them we have no means

73. A Scottish kinglist

dalsi sonuar ludiorum occisus est
in buchain. Lulach fatuus filius maelo
lani regnavit v. annis. fochach [illegible]
[illegible] in igneum cammasium [illegible]
sui [illegible] in quo ingressus habuit [illegible]
[illegible] ubi cecidit duchad
albas duncalden et dubdon sa
trapas atho chlach expulsus
ingressus de regno et tenuit caml
[illegible] tempore domnal filius camll
mortuus est. Culen ring v. a. reg.
martin f. [illegible] dalaig occisus
est in ecclesia sancti michael. leot et
[illegible] exierunt ad romam
maelbrigd episcopus pausavit. cel
lach f. fercalaig regnavit ma
el brigde f. dubican obiit. cu
len [illegible] eochodi occisi sunt
ab [illegible]. Cinadi filius mael
colaim regnavit [illegible] annis. statim predavit
[illegible] ex parte pedestres ci
nadi occisi sunt maxima cede
in [illegible] scotti preda
verunt saxoniam ad stanmoir et ad
[illegible] et ad [illegible] deranu. Ci
nadi [illegible] uallauit ripas uadorum
forthin post annum perrexit cinadi
et predavit saxoniam et tra
duxit filium regis saxonum hic est
qui tribuit magnam civitatem
brechne domino. Cronica regum
scottorum. ccc. xiiii. annorum

Fergus filius erc primus [illegible]
primus qui de semine cho
nare suscepit regnum albanie
i. a monte drumalban usque ad mare
hibernie et ad inchegal iste regnavit
iii. annis. Domangart f. ferg. v. a.
Congel filius domangart. xxx. iii.
Gouerain filius congel. xxii. a.
Conal filius congel. xiiii. a.
Edain filius Gouerain xxxiiii. a.
Eochid buid filius edain. xvi. a.
Kinat sinister filius conal. iii. mensibus
ferchar filius eu xvi annis.
donenald uarius filius eochid. xiiii.
ferchar longus. xxi.
Eochal habens curvum nasum f. do
negarth filii donenal uarii. iii.
Armchellac f. ferchar longi. i. a.
Ewen f. ferchar longi. xiii.
murechat f. armchellac. iii. a.
Ewen f. murcertach iii.
Edalbus f. eochal curvi nasi. xxx
fergus f. hetalbi. iii.
Seluach filius eogan. xxiiii.
Eochal venenosus. f. etalbi. xxx
Dunegal. f. Seluach vii.
alpin. f. eochal venenosi iii.
Kinedus f. alpini primus rex scottorum. xvi
Dolfual f. alpini iiii.
Constantinus f. kinet xx.
hed f. kinet. i. an.
Grig f. dunegal. xii.
dunenal f. constantini. xi.
Constantinus f. hed xxv.
malcolm f. dunenald ix.
Indulf f. constantini ix.
Dub f. malcolm. iiii a. et vi mensibus
Culen f. Indulf. iiii. a. et sex mensibus

of knowing, for scarcely one line written in Pictland in Pictish times has survived to be subjected to historical scrutiny. All the evidence we have comes from Iona or other monasteries of the Irish church and is enough to show that the political reality was the province and its ruler. The province was the limited area within which one man and his retinue could keep some kind of peace, and could control feuds by personal effort, a task which one man alone could not discharge throughout the Pictish regions.

The home of one of these provincial rulers was probably a dun, a promontory or hilltop such as that at Dundurn, situated in the very heart of Scotland but overlooking a route for the Scots to enter Pictland. Someone of great importance, surely a provincial ruler, controlled and commanded many men here, ordering the ditches to be dug and stone for the ramparts to be dragged some fifteen kilometres and, with timber, pulled up the steep hillside.[5] When one of these provincial kings subdued others and became over-king, he created the appearance of a single Pictish kingdom; but what did it amount to in practice? Government, courts or taxes did not exist except in a primitive provincial context. The most significant right of the king of Atholl, to whom Dundurn perhaps belonged, was to call out the host – lord and peasant alike – from his own and tributary provinces. With these men, he could make war on other provinces or neighbours as did the best known of the over-kings, Angus, son of Fergus.

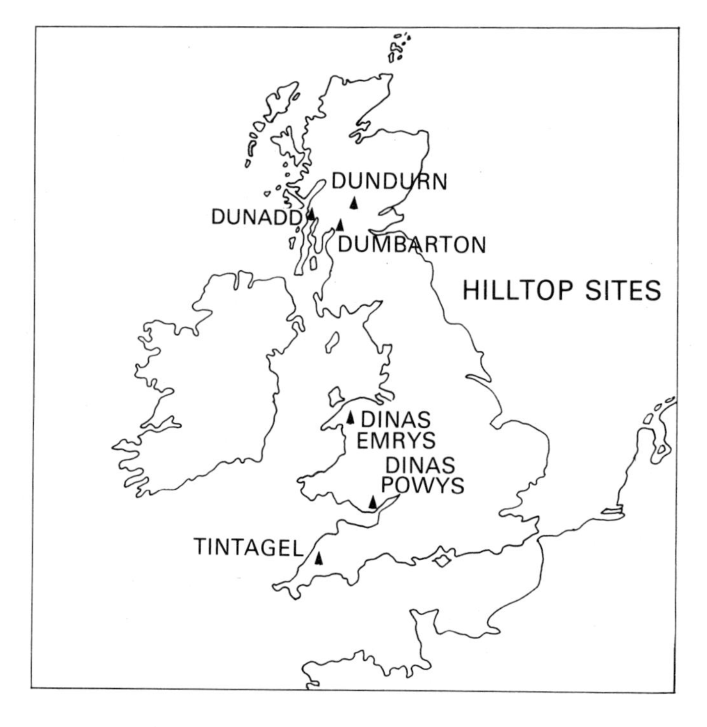


74. Hilltop sites

By 730, Angus had fought his way to hegemony over the bodies of other provincial rulers and their henchmen, some killed in battle, some imprisoned in chains, a few thrown to death by drowning. But in 750 his power waned after the Picts were defeated by the Britons of Strathclyde.[6] Royal power was thus precarious, dependent above all on success in battle which brought riches to the king and his followers. Failure meant no more plunder and rewards in land and consequently desertion by the followers. But success could consolidate success and build towards permanence – a united Pictish kingdom. By the year 800 this process was well under way.[7]

To the Pictish kings extending their rule, another province to subdue was that of the Scots. Their province in the west was relatively weak and made weaker still from 794 when it came under attack from the north and west by the Vikings. At first, the vulnerable kingdom of the Scots seemed destined to be divided between these two forces but, in the event, the fortunes of the Scots were reversed in a most surprising manner.

In 839 the Pictish king was killed by the Vikings and his hegemony broke up in civil war. Among the Scots, Kenneth, son of Alpin, made himself king and with his followers he destroyed, probably piecemeal, the rival Pictish kings. By 850 he was king of the Picts and ruler of all northern peoples. We know the name of no battle in this process, and there is disagreement about whether Kenneth's father Alpin was of the old Scottish royal house or an able adventurer who seized an empty throne. There is, moreover, quite another interpretation of the years 780–850 whereby the Pictish and Scottish royal families intermarried, giving each family a claim on the other family's throne. For example, in this case, Kenneth's mother would have been a Pictish lady. Even in this 'Bourbon and Hapsburg' view of the ninth century Kenneth still won his kingship of the Picts by battle.[8]

Was Kenneth the first king of a united Scotland? The phrase is an anachronism. In the first place his rule stopped at the Forth; and as for a union of the Picts and the Scots, what does that mean? Kenneth took tribute from both, gathered warriors from both and led them into raids on the English, but any idea that he made them conscious of unity would be untimely. He was called King of Picts because his wealth in men and tribute came mainly from the Picts, while the islands of his former Scottish kingdom as well as the most northern Pictish province, Orkney, were being raided and settled by the Vikings.

Ironically, it was under the mastery of these Scottish kings that the Picts, as a distinct people, seem to disappear. The reasons for this submergence are not clear. If we say the Anglo-Saxons had submerged the native Britons, we really mean that the British (Welsh) language ceased to be used in England; we no longer believe that the people were killed or driven out *en masse*.[9] Similarly, the disappearance of the Pictish language and its replacement by the form of Irish we call Gaelic does not have to mean a mass Scottish migration among the Picts, but only a migration of farmers and landlords, the dominant members of society. We know little of why or how such a language change takes place, but the place-names beginning with the Pictish element 'Pit' seem to belong to the time and process of change. For, in the great majority of cases, the second part of each Pit name is a Gaelic word or words, as in Pitlochry, where 'lochry' is 'the king's stone' in Gaelic. It looks as though Pictish 'Pit' remained in use through a period of bilingualism as Gaelic speech spread.[10] But although we know that Gaelic was in general use by the eleventh century, we do not know how long its spread took. Perhaps we have been led by the linguistic change to overestimate the importance of a single kingship over Picts and Scots. Nevertheless, for convenience we can call these lands the Scottish kingdom.

In the past, the Pictish kings had attacked the English in Lothian. Now Kenneth MacAlpin assaulted that province with renewed vigour, as though hungry for yet more territory. At first, it seems likely that the Scottish attacks were no more than robbing and rustling raids of the traditional kind, especially since the great rock fortress of Edinburgh did not fall to the Scots until 960. However, it was the ultimate success of the Scottish kings in extending their rule southwards, not the so-called unification of the Picts and Scots, that was the important, and perhaps surprising, change in this period.

This southern expansion was across a great geographical barrier where the island of Britain is so narrow that it can most naturally be divided in two. Here the Firth of Forth, the Scot-water or Scottish Sea as it was once called, probes deep into the land mass where it becomes a broad moss, an impassable bog until modern times. The only way for invaders to get across this barrier and into Scotland was to capture the one crossing point of Stirling, so it formed a natural frontier between peoples, Picts, or now Scots, to the north, Britons and Angles to the south. Ask Kenneth MacAlpin where England stretched to, and he would have pointed to Edinburgh or Stirling. Yet two hundred years later his successor would have pointed at the Tweed, with a hungry glance at the Tyne, for the hybrid Scottish kingdom, lacking geographical or ethnic unit, had already come into being. Britain was not to be two countries and cultures, one English England, the other Gaelic Scotland, divided at the Forth, but two English countries each with a dissident Celtic culture, the Gaels in Scotland, the Welsh under English rule, and perhaps each the richer in culture for that diversity.

This situation came about because Viking settlers at York destroyed the ancient kingdom of Northumbria leaving a diminished and much weakened Northumberland north of the Tees, isolated from the Anglo-Saxon kings in the south. To unify the kingdom of England, the English kings had to eliminate these Norse rulers. At one point in the 930s the Vikings, Britons and Scots joined forces against the English king. Although Athelstan defeated the coalition in 937, the English kings thereafter thought it wiser to buy the neutrality of the Scots. For a part or all of Lothian, or a part of Cumbria, the Scottish kings were induced to bow the knee in homage to the English king, giving in effect an assurance that he could subdue the Vikings of York without interference from the north.

These English kings, based far away in Wessex, gave away what was not theirs, for little permanent return. By 1018 it was pretty clear that they had lost all chance of ruling beyond the Tweed. This was Lothian, not yet Scotland, but the land of the king of Scots. Of course, there was no reason why he should rule northern Englishmen between Forth and Tweed only, and throughout the eleventh century the Scottish kings harboured hopes of further expansion, bringing their wild followers across the Tweed to plunder and kill in northern England, though without adding an inch of Northumberland permanently to their kingdom.

So slim are our sources that we know of these kings almost solely as war-leaders. They came from one kingly family whose main branches maintained a balance through the acquisition (in about 890) of the ancient British kingdom of Strathclyde which they used to buy off the alternative royal branch. In effect, as each sub-king in Strathclyde succeeded to the throne of Scotland, he appointed his Scottish predecessor's son to Strathclyde. In the 960s impatience and the claims of a third branch brought the system into difficulty. King Dubh, descendant of one son of Kenneth MacAlpin, failed to appoint to Strathclyde the alternate line (descendant of another son) which had preceded him on the throne, and allowed a nearer cousin to become sub-king. For forty years, up to 1005, the various branches of royal kin fought and murdered for the throne, competing for the loyalty of the provincial magnates, and especially the 'great steward' or master of each province.[11] King Dubh's branch ultimately lost out in this struggle for his son was the last of his line to become king. This line perhaps settled for the 'great stewardship' of Fife, for the medieval earls of Fife called themselves the kin of mac Duff, the son of Dubh (which is the remote historical basis for Shakespeare's Macduff).

Historians do not thank Shakespeare for his version of eleventh century Scotland. Almost everything in *Macbeth*, the witches, Duncan's murder, Banquo and Fleance, Macduff, Dunsinane and Birnam Wood, is total fiction, taken over wholesale by Shakespeare

75. Sueno's Stone

and Holinshed from a work by a mendacious University principal. He wrote it in the 1520s to flatter the Scottish king and his nobility with a highly rhetorical pseudo-Livy history, some of which is remarkably reluctant to lie down today. The facts we have are a teaspoonful compared with Shakespeare's bucket, but they do suggest that the eleventh century shows a political advance on the tenth century, in that kingship became relatively stable.

Only Duncan I (1034–40) had a short and unsuccessful reign after his grandfather, Malcolm II, had wiped out all potential rivals in the royal family during a long and successful reign (1005–34). Duncan was killed in battle by a non-royal Macbeth who seized the throne. Although Malcolm II, Macbeth and Malcolm III (Canmore), his successor, won their thrones by killing their predecessors in battle, quite clearly they sat more securely upon the throne than did most later-tenth-century kings. Thus, like Canute, Conrad I, and other ruthless rulers, Macbeth went in piety to Rome to beg pardon for his sins. When he came back after many months he was still king of Scots, a remarkable tribute to his grip upon power. But when he was in Rome he scattered money like seed, we are told,[12] so obviously he had the means of filling his purse and thus buying loyalty.

A government's grip, and that means a king's grip, required one thing – sound and plentiful resources. We can only guess at the ways in which the Scottish king maintained these. The provinces were ruled by mormaers, the equivalent of earls, each with his estates. It may be that this was the patronage through which the king ruled, appointing mormaers, requiring the more distant ones to send him tribute, circulating among those in the eastern lowlands, the area of greatest wealth. Although provincial rivalries persisted and mormaers rebelled, only Macbeth seized the throne, and from the time of Malcolm II kings were generally the masters in their kingdom, perhaps because the ruthless Malcolm in punishing the disloyal acquired much property to reward the loyal. Property meant land, and land furnished two things, army service and rent – in a word, resources.

The career of Dubh is not only instructive but provides uniquely illustrative evidence about army service at that time. Dubh at first beat off a challenge from the collateral heir, whom he had excluded, and who was supported by the men of Athol under the leading churchmen and the mormaer of that province. In 966 the collateral made a second and successful challenge. Dubh was killed at Forres by the men of Moray and the cousin became king; five years later he too was killed and Dubh's brother succeeded. These events must have been made the subject of some long-lost Gaelic epic or lament, of which we hear an echo in a brief Latin annal telling that Dubh lay slain under the bridge of Kinloss and that the sun did not shine until his body was recovered for burial.[13]

However, there are other ways of finding out more about both the king and the society in which he lived. By the road out of Forres to Kinloss there stands a remarkable monument, now badly eroded, with the irrelevant name Sueno's Stone. On one side, carvings depict a great army on horseback. Below, a central figure with a helmet and a quilted coat (Dubh, I suggest) watches with his armed retinue while the armies begin to fight on foot. In the next panel the bodies and severed heads of the dead lie watched over by a church bell and four men with staffs (maybe the clergy), while two couples fight and four men wait to advance with sword and shield. Below that, six of the enemy are fleeing on horseback from a group of eight men armed with swords and shields. But the battle continues with three fighting couples on each side of an arc which is the bridge of Kinloss. Beneath the bridge lie more dead bodies and severed heads; one of the heads, that of Dubh, is framed to stress its importance. At the bottom, the fight continues with one man defending the departure of others.

On the other side, below a great cross, is a badly eroded scene showing four figures bending over a central one; this may represent the burial of Dubh's body, on or near this spot. Only the failure of the sun to shine has defeated the artist in this version of the story, but he depicted, as faithfully as the Bayeux tapestry did later, something of contemporary society. The warriors are simply equipped with sword or spear. The king's retinue have both, and a round shield, and wear unbelted leather coats by way of armour. They are indistinct except in the bottom line where the heads clearly wear helmets of some kind. Some of the men – a wealthier class – are mounted, but the fighting is always on foot.[14] The technology of war is faithfully reproduced here, but so too are the ranks of society and their obligation to fight for a leader.

Army service of this kind is one aspect of a relationship which was widespread in European society: it was owed by those who possessed land and it was owed by them in some kind of proportionality to their land. In other words, these headless corpses represent the farmers or peasants whose labours produced the wealth to support their lords on horseback here, and ultimately to support the king. The other aspect of the relationship is rent. Those who laboured on the estates of great lords – the provincial rulers, abbots and bishops – produced rent in meal, honey and cheese, some of which was paid over to maintain the lord in his hall, doubtless in the same proportions as the military service owed. The rural economy was a struggle to produce food and to maintain the non-producers, the lordly ones riding on their steeds across Sueno's Stone.[15]

With the wealth which they creamed off the rest of society, the greater landowners doubtless commissioned the commemorative stones which continue the Pictish tradition of carving but with declining assurance and skill. These and a very few hoards of buried coins are the only material evidence we have that they were possessed of movable wealth, for no one has identified the homes, halls and storehouses of the men of AD1000. On the one hand there is good evidence of estates comprehending villages and hamlets with ancient names and paying tribute or rent according to long-established formulas. Moreover our Pit names must in any case represent new settlements, new ploughing, new production, the beginnings of an increase in population and a more buoyant economy.[16] Yet on the other hand there is not a trace of the town life such as archaeologists have been busy uncovering in Winchester, York and Dublin. As far as we know Scotland lacked the commerce and industry which require money as a means of exchange. The contrast between England and Scotland in these centuries is a stark one: the English king ruled a country whose vast wealth and developed economy are dramatically illustrated by the huge quantities of coin handed over by Ethelred II to the new Danish attackers, while the Scots king controlled a country with no native coinage and precious little evidence that foreign coins were much used.

But the beginnings of commerce were surely there; we have just not looked long enough or hard enough for them. From its name we can tell that Berwick was once a distant outlying village belonging to some estate, perhaps the estate of Coldingham. But in about 1100 the king took it over and twenty-five years or so later he appointed a sheriff there. Elsewhere the sheriff was the official who handled the meal, fish, honey and cheese which comprised the king's income; he also prepared the king's hall or castle for his visits. But at Berwick these arrangements did not obtain and it seems that the sheriff sold the produce to put cash in the king's pocket, and managed a money economy in what was by now a growing town. This market economy must surely have developed over decades, perhaps even a century, going back to the time of Macbeth. With cash resources on this scale, a king could govern effectively. But Berwick apart, the economy of Scotland and the government of Scotland were backward indeed when compared with those of England, and so too was the intellectual climate represented by the church.

There is nothing more difficult to assess than learning and devotion, for it is typical of human nature that each generation is well satisfied with its own attainment. With hindsight, we can make a simple comparison between two books. The Gospels known as the Book of Kells were probably written at Iona in the eighth century, and are one

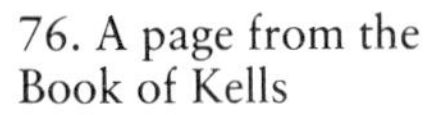

76. A page from the Book of Kells

of the greatest examples of manuscript art. The church among the Scots at that time was surely in some sense learned in the Gospel and lives of the saints and alive to its mission. By contrast another text of the Gospels, the Book of Deer, written in about 1000 in Aberdeenshire, is crudely debased in decoration, the text so garbled as to be useless. However, the manuscript itself is valuable evidence of religious feeling in one respect: the Gospel of St John was well known for its curative powers and in this manuscript it is especially decorated; the book was clearly used to heal the sick.[17] This magical aspect of Christianity was important to a society with no knowledge of medicine or even hygiene. The New Testament tells of and leads the faithful to expect miraculous cures, and the means to these were plentiful. Traditional remedies included sucking a stone washed in a saint's well to cure a fever; wrapping a broken limb in a cloth which has touched the bone of a martyr; and laying St John's Gospel upon an inflammation. Christianity of this kind readily complements the warfare and feud found in Old Testament Judea or MacAlpin's Scotland. So the Pictish kings sought to utilise the powers of the

77. A page from the Book of Deer

apostle Andrew, when some of his bones were brought to a Fife harbour, St Andrews. Kenneth MacAlpin brought the relics, and thus the powers, of Columba from Iona to a new cult centre at Dunkeld, where the humble drank prayerfully at wells and sucked stones. Sometimes they wanted success but most often they sought therapy, as a foundation for their religious life.

There is little sign that lay devotion helped to build either churches or church organisation. One or two church towers seem to come from this period and show that there was some life at monasteries such as Brechin or Abernethy. Interestingly, these two round towers show continuing contact with the Irish Church, though what other forms it took is still unknown.

The Scotland within which one line of kings reigned, and by 1100 ruled, had frontiers established by their efforts, but the subjects within belonged to ethnically disparate peoples, speaking two or three different languages. In about 1125, the sons of Malcolm Canmore spoke of their subjects as 'English and Scots' or 'French, English, Scots and Galwegians'. The land of Lothian was still culturally and even politically distinct from the land across the Scottish Sea, and the land of Galloway in the far south west was even more distinctive through its close links with Ireland. When the unity of Scotland came later through prosperity and firm government, the sense of being one people was buttressed by a mythical history in which the church and its saints played a powerful part. For example, the disciple Andrew became the patron saint. 'Andrew be a leader to us Scottish fellow-countrymen' said the seal which the Scots made for themselves in 1286.[18] But in 1100 the French, English, Scots and Galwegians showed few or no signs of this sense of community or nationhood.

## Further reading

R.A. Dodgshon, *Land and Society in Early Scotland* (Edinburgh, 1981); A.A.M. Duncan, *Scotland: The Making of the Kingdom* (Edinburgh, 1975, reprinted 1978); I. Henderson, *The Picts* (London, 1976); A.P. Smyth, *Warlords and Holy Men AD80-1000* (London, 1984); F.T. Wainwright, *The Problem of the Picts* (Edinburgh, 1955).

CHAPTER ELEVEN

# Myths of the Dark Ages

Janet L. Nelson

Myths, like history, deal with the past, but they deal with it in a very different way. The historian's first aim is to understand the past for its own sake. But the basic function of myth is to give meaning and order to the present. Historians try to be rational and objective. But myths operate at a non-rational level, and are not bound by the evidence of historical reality, even if they often have some historical basis. Every society has its myths and they are part of the education of every child born into it. Modern educators put history, not myths, on the school curriculum. But for most of us, the history we learn in school has quite a lot of myth mixed up with it; there is no harm in this, provided that history teachers are aware of where history ends and myth begins.[1]

People in the Dark Ages had their myths. Tales of heroic ancestors, for instance, expressed and reinforced the identity of a kin-group or a people. Genealogies showing kings descended from gods were manufactured to promote people in power.[2] But such ancient, long-dead myths are not the subject of this chapter. The focus here is on later myths about the Dark Ages – myths that are still alive. First of all, I want to identify the most important myths about this period. Then I shall check them against historians' current picture of Dark Age realities – and I should stress *current* picture, because historians themselves are not immune to myths: that is one reason why history books keep having to be rewritten as each generation revises its perspective on the past.

The first, oldest, and these days the best-known Dark Age myth is the story of King Arthur. We can trace it back to ninth century Wales; but it really blossomed in the twelfth century, in a romance called *The History of the Kings of Britain*, written in Latin by a Welsh writer, Geoffrey of Monmouth.[3] For Geoffrey, Arthur was a British hero who defeated the Saxon invaders of his country. Geoffrey himself was a Briton – a Welsh Briton – writing for Norman lords in the Welsh Marches, an audience glad to hear of the Saxons' defeat centuries before they were beaten again by the Normans in 1066. But this Arthur was more than an anti-Saxon hero. He was also – and this is what supplied his long-term appeal – the greatest warrior ever and a model of chivalry who drew into his service the most valiant knights in Christendom. According to Geoffrey, the wounded but still undefeated Arthur, having beaten the Irish, the Icelanders, the Norwegians, the Gauls and even the Romans, was mysteriously carried off into the sunset. One day, ancient prophecy foretold, he would return. The Arthur myth was a best-seller in the twelfth century. From then on through to the nineteenth century, it was cultivated by aristocrats eager to imitate this model of chivalric virtue. Poets from Malory to Tennyson found Arthur a marketable commodity. And now, in the twentieth century, Arthur has reached a truly popular audience through stage and screen, in *Camelot* and *Excalibur*.[4] The Arthur myth, then, is the first of our myths of the Dark Ages.

The second myth is the myth of Anglo-Saxon freedom. This is the English variant of one of the great universal myths of humankind: the Golden Age before the Fall. Such myths attribute sufferings in the present to particular events in the past; and they offer a message of hope for the future when lost happiness may be regained. The myth of Anglo-Saxon freedom presented the Norman Conquest of 1066 as the Fall from Grace, the source of alien tyranny. Before that, it was alleged, Englishmen were free. They had their own assemblies, or moots, where business was dealt with in their own Old English language, the basis of the English we speak today, and where every free man could have his say. This myth flowered in the early seventeenth century. The opponents of royal absolutism, many of them professional lawyers such as Sir Edward Coke, argued that ancient freedom had not been totally destroyed in 1066: it had survived in the Common Law of England, enshrined in Magna Carta and guarded by the lawyers. And so, before and after the English Civil War in the 1640s and 1650s, many Parliament men demanded the restoration of 'old liberties' and saw themselves as true conservatives.[5] During the Civil War, a group called the Levellers led by John Lilburne put forward a radical version of the Anglo-Saxon myth. They demanded that all laws be issued in English, not in alien French or Latin. They called for a return to what they believed had been the Anglo-Saxon system of government – a decentralised system of local courts where juries of free men declared the good old law without benefit of legal experts. Away with lawyers and judges, greedy professionals! Back to self-government by honest amateurs!

The myth of Anglo-Saxon freedom in its two versions came to embody, during the Civil War, the two main variations of opposition against royal tyranny. The myth became a genuinely popular one. It also had a strong nationalist message: in the seventeenth century, representative institutions were dying out in many parts of Europe, but Englishmen could stand firm in the defence of their freedoms. After the Civil War, the radical version of the myth went underground, to surface again in the writings of Tom Paine in the late eighteenth century and of the reforming Chartists in the nineteenth century. The conservative version flourished as part of a more or less official ideology, 'the Whig interpretation of History', whose theme was the steady progress of the British Constitution towards perfection.[6] Both versions of the myth, despite a decline in popularity during the twentieth century, still have their echoes in the contemporary rhetoric of both Right and Left.

The third Dark Age myth is that of Anglo-Saxon England's unity and independence, of English nationhood created and sustained by Christian monarchy, secured by the invincible English navy, and rooted in a distinctively English culture carried in the English language. This is largely a nineteenth century myth: a myth that could embrace not only all of English-speaking Britain but the whole British Empire, and indeed the whole English-speaking world including the United States of America. It is also in a special sense a Victorian myth. Queen Victoria and her husband Prince Albert shared their contemporaries' interest in the Anglo-Saxon past.[7] In the design of statues in their burial-place at Frogmore, near Windsor, Victoria chose to be commemorated in the guise of Anglo-Saxon royalty. Here Albert calls to mind the central figure in the myth of Anglo-Saxon national identity – King Alfred the Great.

Alfred had been a model of virtuous kingship in the High Middle Ages: the famous story of the burning of the cakes dates from about the year 1100, and was intended to show, for a monastic audience, an example of personal Christian humility. In the late Middle Ages, Alfred's reign was idealised as a time of good government and good laws. The first modern biography of Alfred, already giving him the title 'Great', was written at the outset of the Civil War in the royalist camp at Oxford.[8] But the heyday of the Alfred story as an official, national myth was certainly the nineteenth century. We can trace its growing popularity through the Victorian period. For Alfred's life was celebrated in a series of thousand-year anniversaries that fell, coincidentally, during Victoria's reign. Alfred had been born in Wantage in Berkshire in 849: in 1849 a large number of distinguished people met at Wantage and decided to support what for its time was a

78. Queen Victoria and Prince Albert depicted as a Saxon king and queen in the Mausoleum, Frogmore

large-scale research project on Alfred's reign.[9] In 1871, exactly a thousand years after Alfred became king of Wessex, Thomas Hughes published his *Alfred the Great*. Already famous as the author of *Tom Brown's Schooldays* (which helped create another great English myth

79. Victorian representation of Alfred inciting his troops to victory

– that of the public school), Hughes wrote his biography of Alfred for a popular audience, as 'an Englishman for Englishmen'. Alfred's 'simple, honest life' seemed 'the beginning of all true order for Europe and America'. Hughes' *Alfred* was reprinted no fewer than seven times before 1900, successfully popularising its Anglo-Saxon myth and also influencing the English historians of the late nineteenth century who were laying the foundations of modern Dark Age scholarship.[10]

Alfred died in 899: the millenary of his death was marked by celebrations on a national scale. At Winchester where Alfred was buried, a huge statue was erected in the presence of dignitaries from the Empire and from the United States. In delightful pageants, the local townspeople enacted what were thought of as Alfred's two main achievements: his winning of national victory over the invading Danes, and his nationwide programme of Christian education for the youth of England. Lord Rosebery, the former Prime Minister, imagined Alfred returning to:

> the London he had reconquered from the Vikings . . . then sailing down the imperial river and seeing the British fleet, the offspring of his own poor ships, charged with the wardship of a fifth of the

> world, the traditions of victory and supremacy, and not unequal to the trust.[11]

80. Manuscript showing peasants at work

These then are the three Dark Age myths: Arthurian chivalry; individual freedom; and Alfredian nationhood. How far do these myths reflect the reality of England in the Dark Ages?

In the first case, the Arthur story, the answer is simple: it is pure fiction. It illustrates beautifully the aristocratic tastes and values of the twelfth century when the myth was elaborated; but it tells us nothing about the period around AD500 when Arthur was supposed to have lived. The Arthur story is best left to the literary critics.

For historians, the myth of Anglo-Saxon freedom is more interesting. Half a century ago, the theory of primitive democracy among the Anglo-Saxons still had passionate scholarly champions. Few have much time for it nowadays. It always jarred with the evidence of the early Anglo-Saxon laws with their sharp distinction between the status and power of nobles on the one hand, and peasants on the other, an opposition made neatly in Old English: *eorlas* and *ceorlas* – earls (nobles) and churls.[12] But the notion of primitive democracy has really been discredited by the archaeologists. Excavations in the earliest Anglo-Saxon cemeteries in England have shown that society was already highly stratified in the period of the Anglo-Saxon settlement, the fifth and sixth centuries. There is a great difference, in terms of material goods, between the graves of the rich and the poor: the rich were buried with weapons and ornate jewellery, the poor with at best one or two crude pots.[13] From the later Anglo-Saxon period there is plenty of evidence for a wealthy and status-conscious nobility. According to a late Old English poet:

> Power goes with pride, bold men with brave ones,
> A nobleman goes on the arched back of a war-horse.[14]

And this is how an Anglo-Saxon artist around the year 1000 depicted a troop of noble warriors. From their fortified residences (and again archaeology is beginning to fill out the picture)[15] nobles dominated the surrounding countryside, running the local administration to suit their own interests. The majority of the free population, excluded from warfare and government, laboured on the land – often on other men's land from which they were liable to be evicted for non-payment of renders due. Theirs was a limited and precarious freedom of legal status. They were often compelled by want to sell their children into slavery: although slavery probably declined overall during the Dark Ages, perhaps one in ten of the population was a slave in 1066. In the 1020s the sister of King Canute ran a lucrative white slave trade selling English girls to Scandinavia.[16]

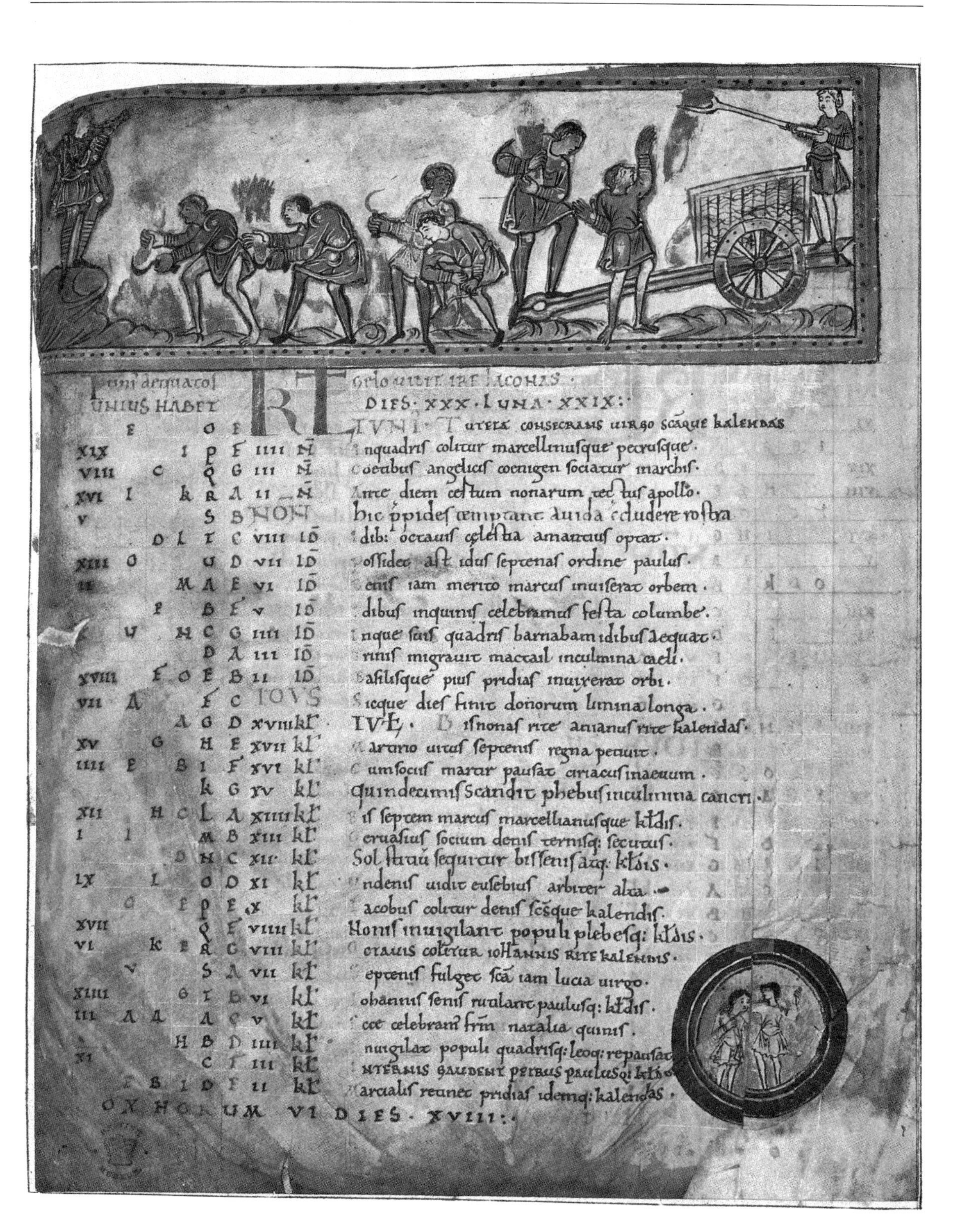

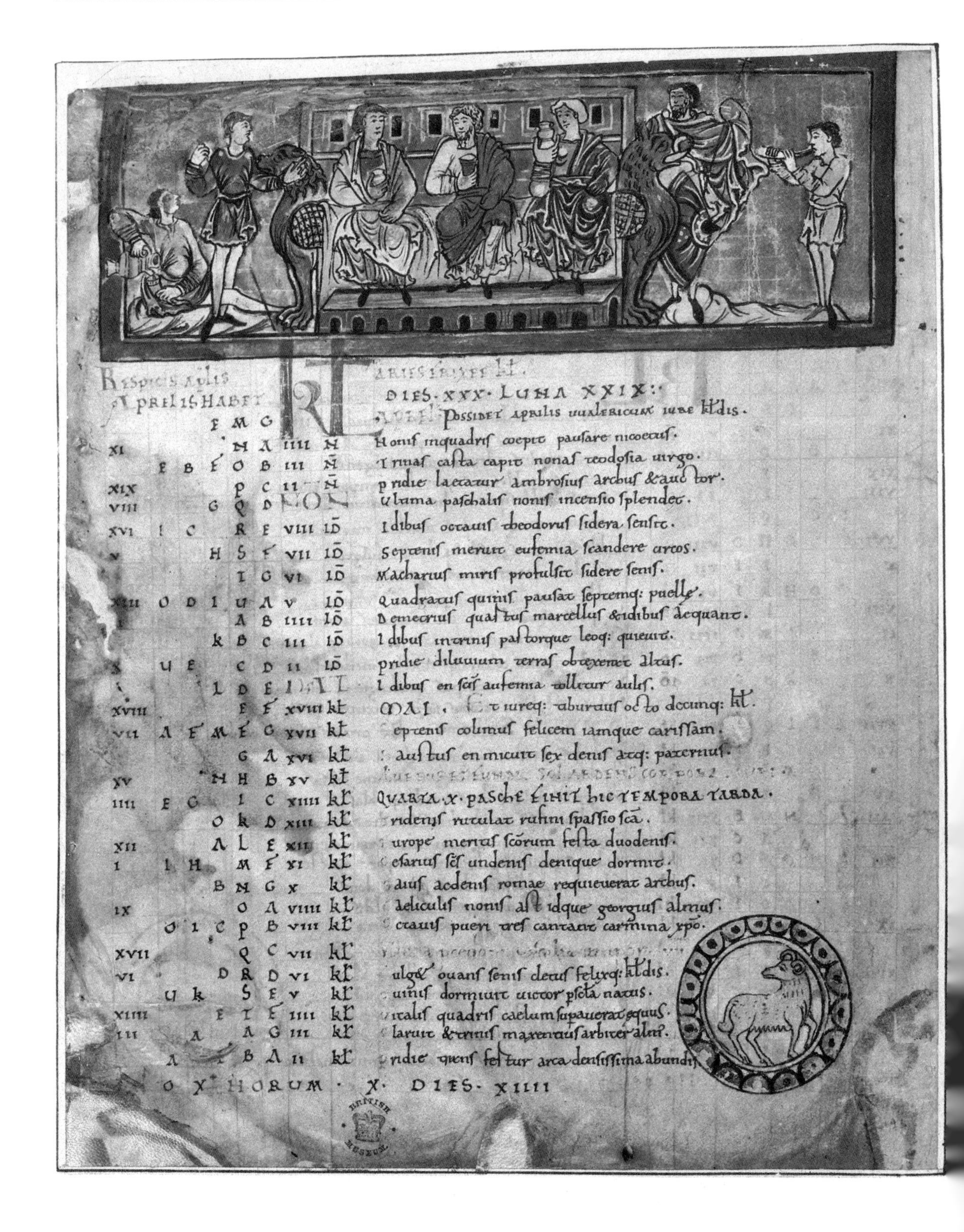

81. Manuscript showing nobles feasting

Anglo-Saxon England, therefore, looks like a hierarchical, oppressive and really very *un*-free society, which would hardly be surprising at this period in European history. But oppression is not the whole story. On a closer look I think the myth of Anglo-Saxon freedom has three quite large elements of truth in it. First, though a wide gulf separated the weak from the powerful, the poor from the rich, that gulf could be bridged by individuals with ability or luck. At the bottom of the scale, slaves were often freed by owners in their wills. The Christian Church exerted a steady pressure against slavery, and the owners sought the good of their souls. The free peasant, the churl, could rise to noble status: according to a legal writer of about the year 1000, a churl who prospered so as to possess a helmet, a coat of mail and a fine sword, a fortified residence and a substantial holding in land, could achieve the legal status of a nobleman.[17] The land was the crucial thing; and it was clearly possible for a peasant through luck of inheritance, or through purchase, to acquire the requisite amount.

At the top of the scale, there was room for new recruits. Viking wars, the subsequent West Saxon expansion northwards, and finally the renewed upheavals of the Danish conquest by King Canute in the eleventh century, all encouraged the growth of a land-market. Old noble families declined; ambitious men, English or Danish, rose, buying their way to status and power – as did Earl Godwin, father of the last Anglo-Saxon king, Harold. Kings would encourage such mobility, as it gave them some freedom of manoeuvre in choosing local officials, and shortened the odds on overmighty subjects.[18]

If social mobility was one kind of freedom, a second was in the area of local government. Free men, provided they had enough land, had the right to attend the local courts of the hundred and the shire, and to have their own cases tried by their fellow-freeholders. They participated in giving judgement. The origins of our jury system lie in groups of twelve such local free men who swore to the truth of the facts in a given case. The direct ancestors of that peculiarly English institution the Justices of the Peace lie in the later Middle Ages. But indirectly it too goes back to the late Anglo-Saxon period, for it was then that a system of royal government was established which combined central direction in the appointing and instructing of officers, with active local participation in the keeping of order and the settling of disputes.[19] The combination, though paralleled elsewhere in Dark Age Europe, was unique to England in its continuous, long-term survival. Because of the relatively small size of the late Anglo-Saxon state by comparison with other European kingdoms, communications between royal court and provinces were easier to maintain. A further significant point here, again unusually for this Dark Age period, was the use in England of the vernacular, Old English, as the language of government. People attending courts found business transacted and recorded not in Latin but in a language they could understand. Old English was used for instance in wills and in descriptions of property boundaries, and also in the writs that transmitted royal orders from the king to local courts. Vernacular literacy in late Anglo-Saxon times may well have been quite widespread among the aristocracy, including women – and for lay persons to be literate was very unusual anywhere in Dark Age Europe where the church in the main monopolised learning. Certainly, anyone regularly attending Anglo-Saxon law-courts would have become familiar with the use of written documents.[20]

None of this adds up to democracy in anything like the modern sense. We are talking about an elite, even if it was quite a broad one. But it is still worth stressing the persistence, in a relatively centralised kingdom, of local government in the hands of local property-holders. In this sense the Levellers were right when they appealed to Anglo-Saxon tradition against the tyranny of the centre and to the amateur wisdom of churls against the expertise of lawyers. Something of this tradition survives to the present day in English local government.

The third important area of Anglo-Saxon freedom is that of the rights and status of women. At least among the landed classes, women in the late Anglo-Saxon period had a remarkable amount of legal independence.[21] They could, for instance, bequeath their own property – and about a quarter of the forty or so surviving Anglo-Saxon wills are those of women. The will of a Hertfordshire woman, evidently a widow, called Æthelgifu came to light quite recently in an outhouse on a country estate, and can be dated to about 990. It begins:

> Æthelgifu cyð hire cwide hire cynehaforde ⁊hire hlaefdian ⁊hire freondon . . .
> [Æthelgifu declares her will to her royal lord and to her lady and to her friends . . .][22]

She made bequests to the local monastery of St Albans and also to a number of male and female kin, and to members of her household including three women capable of chanting psalms in memory of her soul. As well as several estates in three counties, Æthelgifu left over sixty slaves, six hundred sheep, one hundred and thirty cattle, a house in London and a large sum of money. A woman could inherit wealth from her own family, and when she married received from her husband a substantial endowment in land and movables. Widows, unless they remarried, kept control of such endowments and over the inheritances of their young children until they came of age. Women

82. Manuscript showing the condition of women in Anglo-Saxon England

could be parties or witnesses in lawsuits. They could fight successful legal battles to retain their lands, as Æthelgifu in her will says she had done, or to alienate them freely against the rival claims of male kin. The Norman Conquest may have brought a decline in such freedoms. And in one major respect the position in the nineteenth century was no better than in the Dark Ages. Until 1883 a married woman had to wait until her husband's death to dispose of property in her own right, just as Aethelgifu had done in the tenth century.

The myth of Anglo-Saxon freedom has turned out to have some truth behind it, perhaps in unexpected ways. Can as much be said for the myth of English unity and budding imperial power in the Dark Ages?

The Victorians fashioned Alfred's kingdom in their own image, and produced some glaring anachronisms. English sea power, for instance,

MESSRS. VICKERS, & SONS & MAXIM'S INVITATION CARD TO THE LAUNCH OF H.M.S. "KING ALFRED"

83. Alfred's contribution to British naval development: a Victorian view

is a development that came much later than the Anglo-Saxon period. Alfred was not the father of the British navy: kings before him had had warships, and the ships built to Alfred's own design were conspicuously unsuccessful. In 896 several of them ran aground in Southampton Water before they could engage the Danes at all. Alfred's victories were fought on land. It is also fair to add that they depended on a good deal of luck. The brunt of the Danish attacks had been carried by the more northerly and exposed kingdoms of Northumbria and Mercia, so to that extent Wessex had an easier defensive task. The political task of gaining West Saxon ascendancy over Mercians and Northumbrians and Danish immigrants was a far trickier matter. Alfred ruled Wessex, not England. And historians nowadays tend to be sceptical about the extent of national unity in the late Anglo-Saxon period. They stress instead the persistence of provincial separatism throughout the Dark Ages and for long afterwards. English unity in 1066 was skin-deep. Hostility to Wessex remained strong in the midlands and the north, and may well have grown stronger than ever amongst the Welsh and Scots as they reacted against West Saxon imperialism.

But in the end, after making all due allowance for the limitations of Dark Age government and the still embryonic state of national consciousness, I am left strongly impressed by the scope of central power in the late Anglo-Saxon state. No other Dark Age kingdom operated a well-controlled coinage system from more than sixty mints (even if their uneven distribution suggests much more intensive royal control in Wessex than further north).[23] Also impressive is the distinctive quality of late Old English culture. No other Dark Age society has left so many and varied written works in the vernacular: poems, books about law, sermons, saints' lives. English literature really does begin in the Dark Ages.[24] Particularly important was Alfred's personal contribution to these developments. Here again myth turns out to have a firm basis in historical reality. Few rulers in any age have pursued as vigorously as Alfred did both 'weal and wisdom' – material wealth and wisdom. He was a great warlord and winner of spoils. In 886 he captured London, a town that was already becoming a commercial centre. Characteristically, he made the most

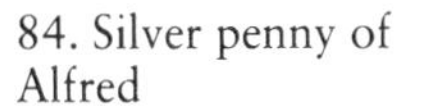

84. Silver penny of Alfred

of this victory by issuing a splendid new coin with the monogram of London on one side and the king's own head on the other. Alfred had a flair for publicity. And his strongest suit was not warfare but conciliation – of Mercians, of Danes, even of Welshmen. Alfred realised that long-term political success depends less on smiting enemies than on winning hearts and minds. He was good at distributing the material benefits that made such success possible. But he was also a persuader and an educator. He drew up a list of books 'most needful for all men to know', and he had these translated from Latin into Old English, and circulated. One such book was the *Pastoral Care*, a book of Christian guidance for persons in authority, written three centuries earlier by Pope Gregory the Great, the apostle of the English. Alfred sent each of his bishops a copy of the Old English version. At the same time he goaded his noblemen into learning to read: when the king himself provided the reading materials, aristocratic literacy could be politically useful.[25]

Alfred promoted, in writing, some myths of his own: the myth of his royal anointing at the age of five by the pope in Rome – a clear sign of divine approval for himself and his descendants; the myth of almost total defeat by the Danes during the winter of 877-8, followed by Alfred's near miraculous victory; and finally the myth of a collective English identity and past, 'happy times throughout England', which Alfred himself was striving to restore.[26] These myths had only a limited foundation in reality. But they helped to create the new realities of the late Anglo-Saxon period: a measure of political and cultural unity for all 'Englishkind'.

I began with the importance of distinguishing clearly between history and myth and the usefulness of having historians capable of making the distinctions. I end with the effect of myth on history. The seventeenth century philosopher Thomas Hobbes saw how this worked: 'No man can have in his mind a conception of the future, for the future is not yet. But of our conceptions of the past, we make a future.'[27]

## Further reading

J. Campbell *et al.*, *The Anglo-Saxons* (Oxford, 1982); Geoffrey of Monmouth (trans. L. Thorpe), *The History of the Kings of Britain* (Harmondsworth, 1966); P.H. Sawyer, *From Roman Britain to Norman England* (London, 1978); M. Wood, *The Dark Ages* (London, 1982).

CHAPTER TWELVE

# The Feudal Kingdoms of Europe

Philip Dixon

When all other dates have faded from memory, one date is likely to remain – 1066, thought by some to be the only date in English history worth remembering. 1066 was an eventful year. The new king, Harold, with troubles in the Welsh west and the Danish north, found himself confronted in the space of a few weeks by an army of Scandinavians near York – this was the last real Viking invasion of England – and he finally fell victim, near Hastings, to a continental adventurer, backed up by the ruffians of Europe and a flag sent by the pope.

Duke William's victory at Hastings was a crucial event in the history of Britain. After 1066 we see a recognisable medieval land, with its churches and castles, villages and manors, lords and peasants. New men had taken over, and they established a social system quite novel in Britain – one which at every point reminds us of its continental origin. But what happened after the Conquest is of no concern to us at the moment. In the following pages, I want to look at the two societies, English and Norman, which came into conflict in 1066, and to show how each had been developing along a separate path.

To understand the extent of the change brought about by the Conquest it is necessary to go back two and a half centuries, to the heyday of the Carolingian Empire. The kingdom of the Franks, like those of the other German peoples who had conquered parts of the Roman Empire, had begun in the fifth century with a king, his tribal aristocrats and warriors, and a subject populace in the ruins of the

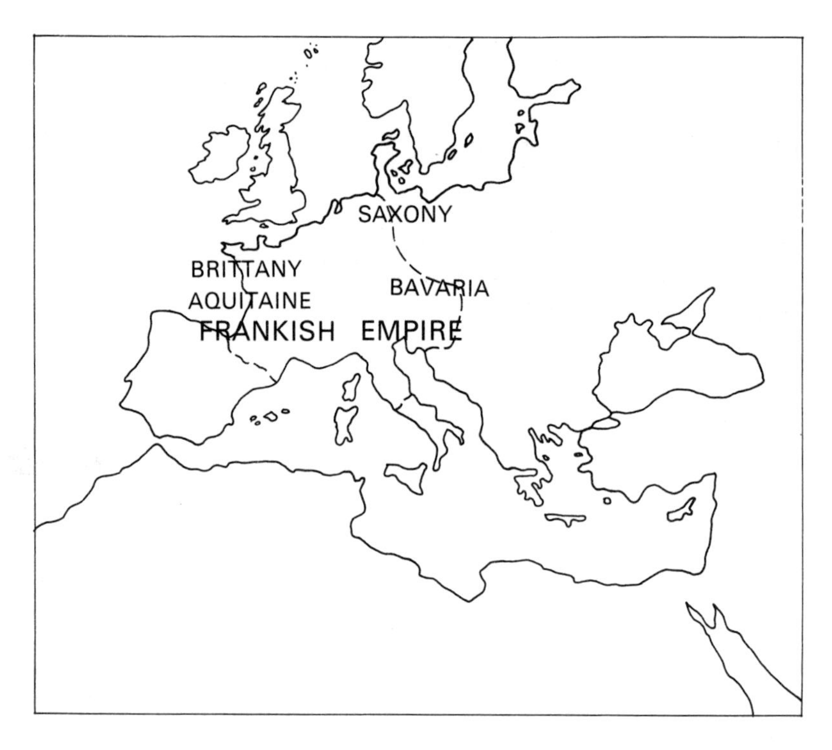


85. The Frankish Empire

civilisation of former Roman provinces. Thanks to the fertility of the land and the success in battle of generations of its kings, the Frankish kingdom grew from its origins in Belgium and the Rhineland to dominate Western Europe, and extended its borders well beyond the area of modern France.[1] The most famous of the Carolingian kings was Charles the Great – in Latin *Carolus Magnus* or Charlemagne – and towards the end of his long reign he and his courtiers began to foster the notion that the barbarian kingdom of the Franks was by now a new empire. The climax came in AD800, when Charlemagne himself was recrowned in Rome, as Emperor of the Franks. By then he had built himself a huge palace complex at Aachen, to the west of Cologne. North of the Alps it was the single largest building programme since the end of the Roman Empire.[2]

These promising beginnings soon came to an end. Charlemagne's empire differed from that of the Romans in several important ways. It had no standing army, just the king's retainers and the Frankish freemen. Their obligations for military service were tribal in origin, and provided an army which was slow to mobilise, proved cumbersome in practice and was normally not available during harvest. The empire's tax system was rudimentary, and its bureaucratic system was in its infancy. In consequence, the kingship was very personal, and there was nothing that would allow the state to survive

86. Model of the palace complex at Aachen

the reign of an inadequate king, or permit a merely competent king to compel the obedience of his distant subjects without the bother of a full-scale military operation against them. This was an important issue in an empire which included independently-minded peoples such as the inhabitants of Brittany, Aquitaine, Saxony or Bavaria. The emperors themselves increased their problems by continuing the age-old inheritance customs of the Franks. When the king had several sons, each took a share of the kingdom. This system, more suited to the running of a farm than an empire, caused family quarrels between the rival heirs which were sometimes settled on the battlefield.[3]

Charlemagne had intended to divide his kingdom between his two elder sons, but they died before him. His surviving son, Louis the Pious, made several attempts at partition, but each attempt was frustrated by the dissatisfaction of the participants. In 833, indeed, his three elder sons captured and imprisoned him. After his death in 840, the brothers fought each other to a standstill, and in 843 they came to

87. Charlemagne

an agreement that each should control the territory he held when the fighting stopped. The consequent separation of the Frankish kingdom into Austrasia (Germany), Neustria (France) and Lotharingia (Alsace-Lorraine and Italy) remained a real division for many centuries.

The internal rivalry of the Frankish kingdom, and the well-developed separatist tendencies of its constituent parts, were destructive. From the 830s onwards, the confusion was greatly increased by

88. The Viking invasion of Normandy

the inroads of a new enemy, the Vikings. These sea-borne raiders were able to make surprise attacks on their victims, then left before help could be brought from the surrounding countryside. From the 840s, therefore, we have the startling picture of the empire, which had crushed opposition on land throughout Europe, falling apart through the pinpricks of small bands of pirates. During the civil wars between Louis and his sons a Danish fleet destroyed the principal trading post of the north, Dorestad, on the Rhine, and for over forty years the Danes dominated the seaways of Frisia. In the 840s, the Vikings burnt the ports of the Seine and Loire, and sacked Hamburg and Paris. By the middle of the century, the pirates were settling down in suitably strong sites such as the island of Noirmoutier off the mouth of the Loire.

The ravages of the Vikings were augmented by those of Arab pirates in the Mediterranean, raiders who in the ninth century conquered Sicily and established a base at St Tropez, near Nice. Rome itself was pillaged in 846, and for a generation the Frankish rulers of Italy were too concerned with self-defence to worry about the politics of the lands north of the Alps. As pressure from the Scandinavians and Arabs slackened, a further threat developed when a group of nomads, called Magyars, settled in Hungary at the end of the ninth century.[4] The Magyars were horsemen, and like the sea-borne Vikings could travel faster than the news of their arrival. In this situation the important man was not the distant emperor but the man on the spot, the local count, who was normally the head of one of the three hundred or so hereditary aristocratic families who were descended from the leading warriors of the Frankish kingdom.

In the face of this pressure, the empire disintegrated into dozens of units, each aware that it belonged to a greater whole, but effectively controlled by the head of its principal noble family. He may have been a count, or occasionally a more important figure, a 'general' (*dux* or duke). The border lands had their 'Counts of the Frontiers' (in German *markgraf*, hence marquis). A duke was more important than a count, and a *markgraf*, through his exposed position, was more independent in action. The one thing they had in common was that as their own power grew, the freedom and power of the kings shrank, until even a strong king found it difficult to control the whole kingdom. In consequence, after the 880s, the north of the Frankish empire split into two realms ruled by a count of Paris and a duke of Saxony, whose successors eventually became kings of France and Germany, and who were sometimes helped and sometimes hindered by the ambitions of their own mighty subjects, their subordinate counts. At the same time a determined group of Vikings turned their attention to the mouth of the Seine where they raided and pillaged with some success until 911, when Charlemagne's great-great-grandson gave them the land they had seized, and made their leader Count of Rouen. The Vikings settled down here. A study of the place-names of the north French coast shows a cluster of Scandinavian names between Rouen and the Channel coast, and by the beginning of the eleventh century, this district and the lands to the west towards Brittany were being called the 'land of the Northmen' – *Normannia* or Normandy.[5]

During these troubled years the upper ranks of society in both France and Germany were changing and reforming into the system which we call feudalism.[6] Its basis was the fee or fief, a piece of land given by the lord of the land to another man, in return for the obligation of military service on the lord's behalf. Some of the characteristics of feudalism can be found at earlier periods: entering into a bond of service, for example, is known from the Carolingian Empire when the procedure comprised a formal ceremony called homage, in which the inferior man (the vassal) placed his hands together between the hands of his lord, quite literally putting himself into the lord's hands. The lord then undertook to protect him, and may also have made some provision for food or land. The ceremony continued into the Middle Ages as an integral part of feudalism.

Another strand in the feudal system was the growing need for professionalism among warriors, a need which arose from the increasing use of horses in war, and the swiftness of sea-borne attacks. One may, perhaps, be a part-time footsoldier (as the German freemen were, in their tribal armies). It is altogether a different thing to be a part-time cavalryman, for horse and rider need regular training to be effective, and the cost of providing each soldier with several horses and their equipment has always made cavalry regiments expensive. The result was that the new mounted soldiers (in German often called *Cnichts*, youths) were unable to maintain themselves: they needed to be supported with enough land to provide them with food, armour, horses, and the luxuries normally demanded by a military elite.[7] The lord who wished to employ the new troops could pay for them from his income and keep them as his household. But normally he chose to find estates for them from his own lands, and in so doing established a class of men who were no longer his hired or sworn retainers. These knights had an overriding obligation to provide military service and

89. Mounted soldiers

they held the lord's land, their knight's fee, as tenants, but otherwise they had some independence.

A further element of the feudal pattern – the castle, or private fortified residence – emerges in the tenth century. It was a response to those unsettled times during the Carolingian collapse when even a strong nobleman might find his household soldiers were unable to protect him unless helped by earthworks and strong walls. The early feudal castle was big enough to be a dignified residence but small enough to be defended by only a few men.[8]

Estates, knights and castles are significant elements in feudalism. The final ingredient that gave the system its particular flavour was the local bias of defence in this period: the knight service owed by the vassal was to his immediate lord, with whom he had struck the bargain of homage. The lord himself might be the vassal of a greater lord, and so on up the social scale to the king, who was the overlord of all other lords in his kingdom. In the older system of the Germanic kingdoms military service was due to the king alone. He was advised by his magnates, of course, but it was quite a different matter when the magnates were the intermediaries of soldiers' loyalty, as they were under feudalism. Profits for the magnates could be considerable. If the lord owed the king the service of twenty knights for his lands, he could retain the land and pay for the upkeep of twenty knights himself. However, it was more common to allocate parts of the fief to others who would then in return provide for the twenty knights. Now, since there was no fixed area of land which provided for a knight, it would be possible for the lord to allocate land in return for the services of not twenty, but twenty-five or thirty knights from among his vassals, giving him, not the king, a surplus of five or ten knights, whose service might from quite early times be converted into cash payments. With his retainers and vassals, it was possible for a strong count to oppose his sovereign's wishes, or even to go to war with him. So feudalism could foment internal wars and diminish the king's authority over the greater lords' territories.

But lords only rarely opposed the king, and of much greater importance for the stability of Europe was the fact that the feudal bond was a service contract that ended with the death of the participants. At first there was no hereditary principle. At the death of the vassal the fief reverted to the lord, who might (at a price) grant it to the vassal's son. However, there was no obligation to do so, and the system must have wonderfully concentrated the minds of vassals on loyalty and service. It put tremendous patronage in the hands of the king, the feudal overlord, and in an age when even aristocrats normally died in their thirties, royal income was greatly augmented by 'reliefs', the money paid to the king by vassals on taking over their estates. For a long time the two systems coexisted: the hereditary counts continued in power while their followers held feudal fiefs. Gradually, each took on aspects of the other. Counts accepted knighthood, even though in other respects they remained a distinct elite at the top of the social pyramid, while the loyal members of the new feudal caste might expect to hand down their fiefs to their heirs. By the eleventh century even the greatest man might become a knight. In the Bayeux tapestry, Duke William can be seen conferring arms on his guest, Earl Harold Godwinsson, shortly before the invasion of England that brought them into conflict.

The feudal society I have been discussing comprised only a tiny fraction, perhaps five per cent, of the population. For most people the changes in society meant only minor changes in their burdens. Their job, under whichever regime, was to work the land and carry out on demand the requirements of either the old or the new customs. But it was they who engendered the wealth which was channelled in different directions by the changing social structures. They formed the enormous mass at the bottom of the social pyramid.

The Northmen who settled in Normandy adapted their customs in accordance with those they found in the new lands. They took up Frankish speech, were converted to Christianity, and absorbed the principles of feudal society from their Frankish neighbours. In a short time they began to prosper. In part this was due to Normandy's favourable position. This was an age when a neighbouring state was very likely to be hostile: a Greek proverb of the time says 'If a Frank is your friend, then he is not your neighbour.' It was thus a considerable advantage for the Normans to have the sea as a safe neighbour to the north. From the sea came trade, especially from England, and the excavations of Anglo-Saxon towns, such as Southampton, have shown that trade with Normandy was increasing in the tenth and eleventh centuries.[9] In both countries towns were growing and revenues were multiplying. In Normandy new monasteries were founded, and even a planned town, the city of Caen, was built.[10] For a long time (over a century) Normandy proved politically stable, and a succession of strong counts managed to tread the narrow path between losing the support of their followers and allowing those followers to develop too much independence.

The contrast between the Continent and Britain at this time is very striking. Some things, of course, were similar: the land was prosperous and towns and trade were developing, possibly a little more slowly in Britain than on the Continent. But in Anglo-Saxon England there was no trace of feudalism. The free Anglo-Saxons and Anglo-Scandinavians had ancient obligations to serve in the army for short periods or to contribute labour to public works. Co-ordination was in the hands of the earldormen, who might become dynasts but whose office was given by the king. Military service was still due to the king directly.[11] There was no cavalry warfare, and even a nobleman, although he might ride to battle, dismounted when he wanted to fight. Without knights, therefore, there was no need for a system of fiefs, and even after two decades of investigation the sites of remarkably few pre-Conquest castles have been found.[12] In short, in Anglo-Saxon England there was no trace of feudalism. One reason is likely to be that the Viking take-over of the various kingdoms of England was so quick that there was no time for centres of local power to develop. In the Carolingian Empire, however, some eighty years of raiding passed between the first attacks and the take-over of Normandy; in this period the continental aristocracy, with its new armies and developing fortifications, made itself independent and powerful.

In England, after the first intermittent raids, the kingdoms fell swiftly into the hands of the Great Army – Northumbria was taken after 866, Lindsey (Lincolnshire) and East Anglia by 869. Mercia fell in 873-4, and by 874 the Vikings were partitioning the newly conquered territory. Wessex, however, survived under Alfred's direct control, and the subsequent reconquest of the Danelaw of Eastern England was under royal supervision. The overall authority changed hands, but Alfred's descendants retained the old system of control through the earldormen. When fresh Viking raids began at the end of the tenth century, we see many examples of independent and vigorous action by local magnates, but the troops they commanded were their household soldiers and shire militias, whose duty lay in the defence of their own regions. When King Canute succeeded to Aethelred's kingdom, only the earldormanic family of Mercia maintained its position. Even though the provincial governors, the earls whom Canute appointed, were Scandinavians or Englishmen who owed their rise to his favour, the traditional forms of Anglo-Saxon government remained unchanged. There was no room for fiefs or vassalage, and the king's strong forces of household soldiers, or housecarls, ensured conformity.[13] After the death of Canute and his sons, the Anglo-Danish kingdom, intact if not wholly united, passed with little change into the hands of the Anglo-Saxon kings, Edward the Confessor and Harold, son of Canute's earl, Godwine.[14]

If one were to examine the neighbouring realms of England and Normandy in the 1040s, at the beginning of Edward the Confessor's reign, neither would appear to be particularly strong. After the able rule of Duke Richard II, brother-in-law of King Aethelred, his sons Richard and Robert successively ruled Normandy. Both died young and may have been ineffectual. The latter left an illegitimate heir who at his succession – in 1035 – was no more than seven or eight years

90. King Canute

old. He became Duke William II, later known as the Conqueror. The Norman nobles were quick to seize their opportunity to acquire the same independence from their overlord that had been enjoyed by other aristocrats in France for some time. Among the ducal powers now weakened were his rights to control castle-building and to nominate to official positions. There were signs that the duke's own demesne lands were dwindling and with them his ability to reward service.[15] As for England, the ancient Anglo-Saxon kingdom had been forcibly united by conquest. But Edward the Confessor, a king who was seldom decisive, ruled a kingdom whose regions had strong separatist tendencies, and no noticeable eagerness to help each other against aggressors. Moreover, the king, having been brought up in Normandy, had Norman favourites which caused much jealousy.

But when we look at the two antagonists of 1066, many of the advantages lie on the side of the English. They were far more numerous: a total population of about one and a quarter million against a Norman military force of under ten thousand. The country

91. William's army at Hastings

could be mobilised into its ancient militia, the levies by shires, which had been effective against many of the Viking attacks. Despite this, the Normans won. But it is a mistake to look for inevitability in events, even though modern explanations of change tend to be based on the workings of impersonal factors – economic shifts, revolutions in technology or social pressures. Prosperity is, of course, normally a prerequisite for success, but the actions of a single person may be the principal element in an event, even one as momentous as the Norman Conquest.

The important figure of the period is Duke William. After he succeeded to the duchy he escaped several attempts by his barons to capture him or supplant him. He emerged a ruthless man, an opportunist whom even a chronicler of the conquered English could regard with awe:

> King William . . . was a man of great wisdom and power, and surpassed in honour and strength all those who had gone before him. Though stern beyond measure to those who opposed his will, he was kind to those good men who loved God. . . .[16]

In the 1040s he overawed and defeated his rivals; in the 1050s he undertook an aggressive policy against his neighbours, largely to consolidate his own position within the duchy by proving himself a successful lord, and to direct the energies of his vassals outside the duchy. His ambitions provoked unsuccessful attacks by the king of France and the count of Anjou in 1053-4 and 1057, and William emerged from the struggle with his power and abilities confirmed. The magnates who supported him found themselves rewarded with lands and were allowed a (limited) participation in his policies. To an extent unusual in contemporary states, the Norman nobles found themselves directly interested in their ruler's success.[17] In consequence, when William turned his attention to England – looking, quite simply, for fresh fields to conquer – he was able to concentrate the resources of the duchy on a military gamble against a country which was considered a united kingdom more frequently by its southern overlords than by the aristocracy of the North and Midlands.

### Further reading

D. Bates, *Normandy before 1066* (London, 1982); D. Bullough, *The Age of Charlemagne* (London, 1973); P. Lasko, *The Kingdom of the Franks* (London, 1971); D. Talbot-Rice (ed.), *The Dark Ages* (London, 1965).

# Notes

## 1. A Continent in Ferment *Philip Dixon*

1. S.S. Frere, *Britannia* (London, 1978) p. 395; J.C. Mann, *Legionary Recruitment and Veteran Settlement* (London, 1983) pp. 89-92; E. Birley, *Roman Britain and the Roman Army* (Kendal, 1976) pp. 82-4.
2. R. Hatchman, *The Germanic Peoples* (London, 1971) pp. 45-50.
3. Ammianus Marcellinus, *The Histories*, Book 31, ch. 4.
4. P.W. Dixon, *Barbarian Europe* (Oxford, 1976) pp. 16-19.
5. A.H.M. Jones, *The Later Roman Empire* (Oxford, 1964) vol. I, pp. 238-65.
6. D. Bullough, *Age of Charlemagne* (London, 1973) p. 75; P. Grimm, 'The Royal Palace at Tilleda, Kr Sangerhausen, DDR', *Mediaeval Archaeology* XII (1968) pp. 83-100; H.J. Jacobi (ed.) *Die Ausgrabungen in der Königspfatz Ingelheim* (Bonn, 1976).
7. R. Reece, 'Town and Country: the end of Roman Britain', *World Archaeology* 12(1) (1980) pp. 77-92. For a magisterial survey see A.H.M. Jones, op. cit., vol. II, note 5, pp. 1025-68.
8. M.W. Barley (ed.) *European Towns* (London, 1976) pp. 188-90.
9. A.G. Poulter, 'Roman Towns and the Problem of late Roman Urbanism', *Hephaistos* (forthcoming); M. Roblin, 'Cités ou Citadelles', *Revue des Études Anciennes* 67 (1965) pp. 368-91.
10. M. Todd, *The Northern Barbarians* (London, 1975) pp. 95-128.
11. W. van Es, 'Wijster: a native village beyond the Imperial Frontier, 150-425AD', *Palaeohistoria* XI (1967) pp. 531-67.
12. F. Tischler, 'Der Stand der Sachsenforschung, archäologisch gesehen', *35 Bericht der Römisch-Germanischen Kommission* (1954) pp. 168-95.
13. M. Todd, op. cit., p. 195.
14. W. Janssen, 'Mittelalterische Dorfsiedlungen als archäologisches Problem', *Frühmittelalterische Studien 2* (1968) pp. 305-67, especially p. 345.
15. See Chapter 3 for a fuller discussion of Germanic trading links with the empire.
16. G. Haseloff, 'Salin's Style I', *Mediaeval Archaeology* 18 (1974) p. 4.
17. W. Goffart, *Barbarians and Romans* (Princeton, 1980) pp. 206-30.
18. J.M. Wallace-Hadrill, *The Barbarian West* (London, 1967) pp. 24-42.
19. M. Todd, op. cit., p. 19.
20. S. Vryonis, *Byzantium and Europe* (London, 1967) pp. 57-70.

## 2. After the Romans *Malcolm Todd*

1. S.S. Frere, *Britannia: A History of Roman Britain* (London, 1978) p. 376.
2. E.A. Thompson, 'Britain, AD406-10', *Britannia* (VIII) pp. 303-18.
3. Zosimus VI, 10.
4. S.S. Frere, op. cit., p. 387; M. Todd, *Roman Britain* (London, 1981) p. 220.
5. A.L.F. Rivet, *Town and Country in Roman Britain* (London, 1964) pp. 60-71.
6. E. and J.R. Harris, *The Oriental Cults in Roman Britain* (Leiden, 1965).
7. C. Thomas, *Christianity in Roman Britain* (London, 1981) p. 142.
8. M. Todd, op. cit., p. 224.
9. P.A. Barker, 'Excavation at the Baths Basilica at Wroxeter, 1966-74', *Britannia* (VI) pp. 106-17.
10. P. Bidwell, *The Legionary Bath-House and Basilica and Forum at Exeter* (Exeter, 1979) p. 104.
11. S.S. Frere, *Verulamium Excavations*, vol. II (London, 1983) p. 93.
12. L. Alcock, *Arthur's Britain* (London, 1971) pp. 98-108.
13. C. Thomas, op. cit., p. 271.

## 3. The Anglo-Saxon Migrations *Richard Hodges*

1. Bertram Colgrave and R.A.B. Mynors (eds) *Bede's Ecclesiastical History of the English People* (Oxford, 1969) pp. 40-1.
2. H. Ament, 'The Germanic tribes in Europe', in D.M. Wilson (ed.) *The Northern World: The History and Heritage of Northern Europe, AD400-1100* (London, 1980) pp. 49-70.
3. R.E.M. Wheeler, *Rome beyond the Imperial Frontier* (London, 1954).
4. Klavs Randsborg, 'Rank rights and resources: an archaeological perspective from Denmark', in C. Renfrew and S.J. Shennan (eds) *Ranking, Resource and Exchange* (Cambridge, 1982) pp. 132-40.
5. See Klavs Randsborg, *The Viking Age in Denmark* (London, 1980) for a discussion on the climate in the first millennium AD.
6. Boats of this period are discussed in R.L.S. Bruce-Mitford, *The Sutton Hoo Ship Burial, vol. I,* British Museum (London, 1975).
7. Catharine Hills, 'The Anglo-Saxon settlement of England', in D.M. Wilson, op. cit., p. 71ff.
8. J.N.L. Myres, *Anglo-Saxon Pottery and the Settlement of England* (Oxford, 1969).
9. David A. Hinton, 'Hampshire's Anglo-Saxon origins', in S.J. Shennan and R.T. Schadla-Hall (eds) *The Archaeology of Hampshire* (Hampshire Field Club Monograph, 1981) pp. 56-65.
10. Philip Rahtz, 'Buildings and rural settlement', in D.M. Wilson (ed.) *The Archaeology of Anglo-Saxon England* (London, 1976) pp. 49-98.
11. C.J. Arnold, 'Stress as stimulus for socio-economic change: Anglo-Saxon

England in the seventh century', in C. Renfrew and S.J. Shennan, op. cit., pp. 124-31.
12. Margaret Gelling, *Signposts to the Past: Place-names and the History of England* (London, 1981).
13. Charles Thomas, *Christianity in Roman Britain to AD500* (London, 1981).
14. Brian Hope-Taylor, *Yeavering*, HMSO (London, 1977); Rahtz, op. cit.
15. Leslie Alcock, *Arthur's Britain* (London, 1971). See also Chapter 5.
16. F.J. Byrne, *Irish Kings and High Kings* (London, 1973).
17. Jack Goody, *The Domestication of the Savage Mind* (Cambridge, 1977) and idem, *The Development of the Family and Marriage in Europe* (Cambridge, 1983) provide valuable insights into these changing values.

## 4. The Emergence of Anglo-Saxon Kingdoms *Patrick Wormald*

1. Standard edition: C. Plummer (ed.) *Baedae Venerabilis Opera Historica* (2 vols, Oxford, 1896), with priceless commentary; a modern text, with facing translation and short notes: B. Colgrave and R.A.B. Mynors (eds) *Bede's Ecclesiastical History of the English People* (Oxford, 1969); see also *Further Reading.*
2. Most kingdoms are surveyed by F.M. Stenton, *Anglo-Saxon England* (Oxford, 3rd edn, 1971) chs 2, 3; for the multiplicity of kingdoms: J. Campbell, *Bede's 'Reges' and 'Principes'* (Jarrow lecture, 1979).
3. Modern studies of the Mercian kingdom in various aspects: A. Dornier (ed.) *Mercian Studies* (Leicester, 1977).
4. Bede, *Ecclesiastical History*, III 24.
5. Letter of Alcuin to the Mercian ealdorman Osbert, quoted from D. Whitelock (ed.) *English Historical Documents*, vol. I (London, 2nd edn, 1979) no. 202.
6. Standard edition: F. Klaeber (ed.) *Beowulf and the Fight at Finnsburg* (Lexington, 3rd edn, 1950); see also *Further Reading.*
7. *Beowulf*, ll. 2864-91.
8. *Beowulf*, ll. 64-7.
9. See *Further Reading.*
10. See Bede, *Ecclesiastical History*, I 25.
11. The Laws of Ine, no. 70:1, quoted from *English Historical Documents*, vol. I, no. 32.
12. A list of all known Anglo-Saxon royal vills: P.H. Sawyer, 'The Royal *Tun* in pre-Conquest England', P. Wormald (ed.) *Ideal and Reality in Frankish and Anglo-Saxon Society* (Oxford, 1983) pp. 289-99; a spectacular excavated example: B. Hope Taylor, *Yeavering* (London, 1977).
13. For Offa's Dyke and the Tribal Hidage: D. Hill, *Atlas of Anglo-Saxon England* (Oxford, 1981) pp. 75-7.
14. Charter of Aethelbald, King of Mercia, quoted from *English Historical Documents*, vol. I, no. 66.
15. On coinage history: M. Dolley, 'The Coins', in D. Wilson (ed.) *The*

*Archaeology of Anglo-Saxon England* (London, 1976).
16. Hill, op. cit., pp. 120-3.
17. *Beowulf*, ll. 2029-31.
18. Bede, *Ecclesiastical History*, II 5; *Anglo-Saxon Chronicle*, year '829', quoted from *English Historical Documents*, vol. I, no. 1; charter of Aethelbald, King of Mercia, quoted from ibid., no. 67.
19. For a detailed statement of the arguments that follow: P. Wormald, 'Bede, the *Bretwaldas* and the origins of the *gens Anglorum*', op. cit., pp. 99-129.
20. Bede, *Ecclesiastical History*, II 1.

## 5. Picts, Scots and Britons *Wendy Davies*

1. For source material see W. Davies, *Wales in the Early Middle Ages* (Leicester, 1982) pp. 198-218; D.N. Dumville, 'Sub-Roman Britain', *History*, LXII (1977) pp. 173-92; A.A.M. Duncan, *Scotland: The Making of the Kingdom* (Edinburgh, 1975) pp. 636-46; A.O. Anderson, *Early Sources of Scottish History* (2 vols, Edinburgh, 1922); Cf. K. Hughes, *Early Christian Ireland: Introduction to the Sources* (London, 1972); S.M. Pearce, *The Kingdom of Dumnonia* (Padstow, 1978); and C. Thomas, *The Early Christian Archaeology of North Britain* (London, 1971).
2. See W. Davies, op. cit., pp. 67-71; H.M. Chadwick, *The Heroic Age* (Cambridge, 1912).
3. K.H. Jackson, *The Gododdin* (Edinburgh, 1969) pp. 106-7.
4. *Rhigyfarch's Life of St. David*, ed. J.W. James (Cardiff, 1967) chs 21, 30, 31, pp. 12-14, 35-8.
5. See W. Davies, op. cit., pp. 209-12, 207f.; K.H. Jackson, 'The Sources for the Life of St. Kentigern', in N.K. Chadwick *et al.*, *Studies in the Early British Church* (Cambridge, 1958) pp. 273-357.
6. K.H. Jackson, *Language and History in Early Britain* (Edinburgh, 1953); id. 'Angles and Britons in Northumbria and Cumbria', in H. Lewis (ed.) *Angles and Britons* (Cardiff, 1963) pp. 60-84; id. 'The Pictish language', in *The Problem of the Picts*, ed. F. Wainwright (Edinburgh, 1955); W.F.H. Nicolaisen, 'P-Celtic Place-names in Scotland: A Reappraisal', *Studia Celtica*, VII (1972) pp. 1-11.
7. See Chapter 3 for a comparison with the emergence of kings among the Anglo-Saxons in south-eastern England.
8. N. Chadwick, 'Colonisation of Brittany from Celtic Britain', in *Proceedings of the British Academy*, LI (1965) pp. 235-99; L. Fleuriot, *Les Origines de la Bretagne* (Paris, 1980).
9. S.M. Pearce, *Kingdom of Dumnonia*, plate 22a and p. 26.
10. J. Bannerman, *Studies in the History of Dalriada* (Edinburgh, 1974) pp. 1-9.
11. See Chapter 10 for further information.
12. W. Davies, *An Early Welsh Microcosm* (London, 1978) pp. 65-98.
13. See W. Davies, *Wales in the Early Middle Ages* (Leicester, 1982) pp. 85-

102; I. Williams, *The Beginnings of Welsh Poetry*, ed. and trans. R. Bromwich (Cardiff, 1972) pp. 70-88.
14. *Annals of Ulster*, ed. W.M. Hennessy (Rolls Series, 1887) *sub anno* 728.
15. J. Bannerman, *Studies in the History of Dalriada* (Edinburgh, 1974) pp. 27-156.
16. See Chapter 4 and Chapter 10 for more details.
17. W. Davies, *An Early Welsh Microcosm* (London, 1978) p. 43.
18. D. Jenkins and M.E. Owen, 'The Welsh Marginalia in the Lichfield Gospels', pt I, *Cambridge Medieval Celtic Studies*, V (1983) p. 51; see also W. Davies, *Wales in the Early Middle Ages* (Leicester, 1982) pp. 132-4, and *An Early Welsh Microcosm* (London, 1978) pp. 108-20.
19. V.E. Nash-Williams, *The Early Christian Monuments of Wales* (Cardiff, 1950) no. 33; see also W. Davies, *Wales in the Early Middle Ages* (Leicester, 1982) pp. 74f.
20. W. Davies, *Wales in the Early Middle Ages* (Leicester, 1982) pp. 71-81; see also Chapter 3.
21. I. Henderson, *The Picts* (London, 1967) pp. 31-3; A.A.M. Duncan, *Scotland: The Making of the Kingdom* (Edinburgh, 1975) pp. 48ff.
22. I. Henderson, *The Picts* and F. Wainwright (ed.), *Problem of the Picts, Historical Atlas of Scotland c.400-c.1600*, ed. P. McNeill and R. Nicholson (Conference of Scottish Medievalists, 1975) pp. 9-11, 114ff.
23. A.O. and M.O. Anderson (eds.), *Adomnan's Life of Columba* (London, 1961).
24. ibid., p. 369.
25. W. Davies, *Wales in the Early Middle Ages* (Leicester, 1982) p. 67.

## 6. The Christian Connection *Liam de Paor*

1. The early development summarised here is discussed in some detail by Margaret Deanesly, *The Pre-Conquest Church in England* (London, 1961).
2. See, however, the discussion by C. Thomas, 'East and West: Tintagel, Mediterranean Imports and the Early Insular Church' in Susan M. Pearce, ed., *The Early Church in Western Britain and Ireland* (British Archaeological Reports, British Series 102, 1982) p. 17.
3. The main evidence is in the *Chronicon* of Prosper of Aquitaine, ed. T. Mommsen, *Monumenta Germaniae Historica Auct. Antiq. Roman IX (Chronica Minora I)* pp. 353-499.
4. All of this discussion is difficult and controversial. See C. Thomas, *Christianity in Roman Britain to AD500* (London, 1981) for more detail.
5. See F. Henry, 'Early Monasteries, Beehive Huts and Dry-stone Houses in the Neighbourhood of Cahirciveen and Waterville (County Kerry)', *Proceedings of the Royal Irish Academy* 85 (1955) p. 174.
6. A.O. and M.O. Anderson, *Adomnan's Life of Columba* (London, 1961) p. 222.
7. L. Sherley-Price (trans.) *Bede: a History of the English Church and People* (Harmondsworth, 1965) p. 69.

8. L. Sherley-Price, op. cit., p. 127.
9. ibid., p. 86.
10. G.S.M. Walker, *Sancti Colombani Opera* (Dublin, 1970) pp. 24, 25, 38, 39.
11. A.S. Cook and C.B. Tinker, *Select Translations from Old English Poetry* (Boston, 1926) pp. 100-3, quoted in Margaret Deanesly, op. cit., p. 171.
12. Bertram Colgrave and R.A.B. Mynors (eds) *Bede's Ecclesiastical History of the English People* (Oxford, 1969) pp. 16-17.

## 7. The Viking Nation *Klavs Randsborg*

1. D. Whitelock (ed.) *English Historical Documents I*, c.500-1042 (London, 1955).
2. Especially for references to Denmark, see K. Randsborg in *Further Reading*.
3. For the most recent dicussion, see R. Hodges and D. Whitehouse, *Mohammed, Charlemagne and the Origins of Europe: Archeology and the Pirenne Thesis* (London, 1983). See also M. Lombard in *Further Reading*.
4. R. McC. Adams, *Heartland of Cities, Surveys of Ancient Settlement and Land Use on the Central Floodplain of the Euphrates* (Chicago and London, 1981) p. 175.
5. D. Ellmers, 'Frühmittelalterliche Handelsschiffart in Mittel – und Nordeuropa', *Offa-Bücher* 28 (1972) has many further references to the ships.
6. A.S. Ingstad, 'The Norse Settlement at L'Anse aux Meadows, A Preliminary Report from the Excavations 1961-1968', *Acta Archaeologica* 41 (1970) p. 109.
7. O. Frydenberg and J.V. Spärck, *Arv og race hos mennesket* (København, 1963).
8. M. Lombard (see *Further Reading*) has a full discussion of this empire.
9. K. Randsborg, 'Les activitiés internationales des Vikings: raids ou commerce?', *Annales Économies Sociétiés Civilisations* (1981) p. 862.
10. H. Jankuhn, *Haithabu, Ein Handelsplatz der Wikingerzeit* (Neumünster, 1976).
11. Viking ideology and art is dealt with by P.G. Foote and D.M. Wilson, see *Further Reading*.
12. S. Hvass, 'The Viking-age Settlement at Vorbasse, Central Jurland', *Acta Archaeologica* 50 (1979) p. 137.
13. O. Olsen and H. Schidt, 'Fyrkat, en jysk Vikingeborg I. Borgen og bebyggelsen', *Nordiske Fortidsminder serie B, in 4to*, no. 3 (1977); E. Roesdahl, 'Fyrkat, en jysk Vikingeborg II. Oldsagerne og gravpladsen', *Nordiske Fortidsminder serie B, in 4to*, no. 4 (1977).
14. E. Albrectsen, *Vikingerne i Franken* (Odense, 1976).

## 8. The Vikings in Britain *Alfred P. Smyth*

1. P.H. Sawyer, *Kings and Vikings: Scandinavia and Europe AD700-1100* (London, 1982) pp. 90-4.
2. D. Ó'Corráin, *Ireland before the Normans* (Dublin, 1972) pp. 80-110.
3. See, for example, P.H. Sawyer, op. cit.; Alfred P. Smyth, *Scandinavian Kings in the British Isles, 850-880* (Oxford, 1977); P.G. Foote and D.M. Wilson, *The Viking Achievement: the Society and Culture of Early Scandinavia* (London, 1970).
4. Alfred P. Smyth, *Scandinavian York and Dublin: the History and Archaeology of Two Related Viking Kingdoms*, 2 vols (Dublin, 1979) pp. 134-7.
5. Magnus Magnusson and Hermann Palsson (trans.) *Laxdaela Saga* (Harmondsworth, 1969); see also Magnus Magnusson and Hermann Palsson (trans.) *Njal's Saga* (Harmondsworth, 1960).
6. Translated from G. Jónsson and B. Vilhjálmsson (eds.) *Fornaldar Sögur Nordurlanda* (3 vols) (Reykjavik, 1943-4).
7. Translated from F. Hervey (ed.) *Carolla Sancti Eadmundi: the Garland of St. Edmund, King and Martyr* (London, 1907).
8. M. Dolley, *Viking Coins of the Danelaw and of Dublin* (London, 1965) pp. 16-31.
9. Alfred P. Smyth, *Scandinavian York and Dublin* (Dublin, 1979), pp. ii, 191-242.
10. R.A. Hall (ed.) *Viking Age York and the North* (Council for British Archaeology, 1978) gives further details on the excavations in York. See also *Interim: the Journal of the York Archaeological Trust.*
11. D. Whitelock, *The Anglo-Saxon Chronicle (60BC-AD1042)* in *English Historical Documents c.500-1042*, gen. ed. D.C. Douglas (London, 1968) vol. I, pp. 200-1.

## 9. One English Nation *Pauline Stafford*

1. Treaty of Alfred and Guthrum, ch. 1, printed *English Historical Documents*, vol. I, ed. D. Whitelock (London, 1979) p. 416.
2. Florence of Worcester, *Chronicon ex Chronicis*, ed. B. Thorpe (London, 1848-9) *sub anno* 993.
3. *Anglo-Saxon Chronicle*, MS C 1002, *English Historical Documents*, vol. I, p. 239.
4. ibid., p. 591.
5. Fourth code of Edgar, ch. 2.1, *English Historical Documents* vol. I, p. 435, and Third Code of Ethelred, ch. 1.1, ibid., p. 439.
6. See J. Lang, 'Continuity and Innovation in Anglo-Scandinavian Sculpture: A Study of the Metropolitan School at York', *Anglo-Saxon and Viking Age Sculpture*, ed. J. Lang, British Archaeological Reports, British Series, 49 (Oxford, 1978), and R.N. Bailey, *Viking Age Sculpture in Northern England* (London, 1980).

7. *Anglo-Saxon Chronicle*, MS D 948, *English Historical Documents*, vol. I, p. 223.
8. *Anglo-Saxon Chronicle*, MSS D and E 975, *English Historical Documents*, vol. I, p. 228 and S.633 (S + number indicates number in P.H. Sawyer, *Anglo-Saxon Charters, an Annotated Handlist and Bibliography* (London, 1968)).
9. For the career and property of Athelstan, see C. Hart, 'Athelstan Half-King and his family', *Anglo-Saxon England*, vol. II, ed. P. Clemoes (Cambridge, 1973) pp. 115-44.
10. See A. Williams, 'Some notes and considerations on problems connected with the English royal succession, 860-1066', *Proceedings of the Battle Abbey Conference*, vol. I, ed. R. Allen Brown (Ipswich, 1979) pp. 144-67, and P.A. Stafford 'The King's Wife in Wessex', *Past and Present*, no. 91 (1981) pp. 3-27.
11. The Hundred Ordinance, ch. 1, *English Historical Documents*, vol. I, p. 430 and Third Code of Edgar, ch. 5.1, F. Liebermann, *Die Gesetze der Angelsachsen*, vol. I (Halle, 1903) p. 202.
12. A. Robertson, *Anglo-Saxon Charters* (Cambridge, 1956) p. 66.
13. See P.A. Stafford, op. cit., on royal marriages.
14. P.A. Stafford, 'The Reign of Ethelred II: A study in the limitations on royal policy and action', *Ethelred the Unready*, ed. D. Hill, Britishu Archaeological Reports, British Ser. 59 (Oxford, 1978) p. 34, n.103.
15. D.M. Metcalf, 'The ranking of boroughs: numismatic evidence from the reign of Æthelred II', *Ethelred the Unready*, ed. D. Hill, p. 172, and *English Historical Documents*, vol. II, ed. D.C. Douglas and G.W. Greenaway, 2nd edn (London, 1981) p. 877.
16. R.H.M. Dolley and D.M. Metcalf, 'The Reform of the English Coinage under Eadgar', *Anglo-Saxon Coins*, ed. R.H.M. Dolley (London, 1961) pp. 136-68.
17. *Anglo-Saxon Chronicle*, MS C 1012, *English Historical Documents*, vol. I, p. 245.
18. See A. MacGregor, 'Industry and Commerce in Anglo-Scandinavian York', *Viking Age York and the North*, ed. R.A. Hall (London, 1978) pp. 37-57, and *The Vikings in England*, catalogue of the 1982 exhibition, ed. E. Roesdahl *et al.* (London, 1981) for R. Hall, 'The markets of the Danelaw', pp. 95-139.
19. K. Kilmarry, *The Pottery Industry of Stamford,* British Archaeological Reports, British Ser. 83 (1980).
20. See Hart, op. cit., n. 9, pp. 116-20, on the origins of Athelstan Half-King; for Aelfhere see A. Williams, '*Princeps Merciorum Gentis*, the family, career and connections of Ælfhere, ealdorman of Mercia, 956-83', *Anglo-Saxon England*, vol. X, ed. P. Clemoes (Cambridge, 1982) pp. 143-72.
21. D. Whitelock, 'Dealings of the kings of England with Northumbria in the tenth and eleventh centuries', *The Anglo-Saxons*, studies presented to Bruce Dickins, ed. P. Clemoes (London, 1959) pp. 70-88.
22. Fifth Code of Ethelred, ch. 1, *English Historical Documents*, vol. I, p. 442.

23. Northumbrian Priests' Law, chs 54, 13 and 14, ibid, pp. 473-5.
24. F. Barlow, *Eht English Church, 1000-66* (London, 1963) p. 105, and J.M. Cooper, *The Last Four Anglo-Saxon Archbishops of York*, Borthwick Papers 38 (York, 1970).
25. Life of Oswald, *Historians of the Church of York and its Archbishop*, ed. J. Raine, vol. I (Rolls Series 1879) pp. 436-8.
26. D. Whitelock, 'Wulfstan and the laws of Cnut', *English Historical Review*, vol. 63 (1948) pp. 433-52.
27. P.A. Stafford, 'The Laws of Cnut and the history of Anglo-Saxon royal promises', *Anglo-Saxon England*, 10, ed P. Clemeres (Cambridge, 1982) pp. 173-90.

## 10. The Kingdom of the Scots *A.A.M. Duncan*

1. A.O. Anderson, *Early Sources of Scottish History* (Edinburgh, 1922) has all the Irish sources in translation, and his *Scottish Annals from English Chroniclers* (London, 1908) has all the English ones.
2. W.F.H. Nicolaisen, *Scottish Place Names* (London, 1976) pp. 149-59, 164-5.
3. The literature on the Pictish symbol stones is considerable. They are catalogued in J. Romilly Allen and J. Anderson, *The Early Christian Monuments of Scotland* (3 vols, 1903). A useful short introduction is Joanna Close-Brooks and Robert B.K. Stevenson, *Dark Age Sculpture* (Edinburgh, 1982). A more controversial view is that of A.C. Thomas 'The Interpretation of the Pictish Symbols', *Archaeological Journal* CXX (1963) pp. 31-97.
4. M.O. Anderson, *Kings and Kingship in Early Scotland* (Edinburgh, 1973) is an invaluable introduction to the king lists.
5. L. Alcock, *Excavations at Dundurn, St. Fillans, Perthshire 1976-7. An Interim Report* (Glasgow, 1978).
6. The best discussion on Angus is I. Henderson, *The Picts* (London, 1976) ch. 2.
7. See also Chapter 4 for a comparison with the process in England.
8. M.O. Anderson, 'Dalriada and the Creation of the Kingdom of the Scots' in *Studies in Memory of Kathleen Hughes*, ed. D. Dumville *et al.* (Cambridge, 1982) pp. 106-32.
9. See Chapter 3 for further details on the Anglo-Saxon settlement.
10. K.H. Jackson, 'The Pictish Language' in *The Problem of the Picts*, ed. F.T. Wainwright (Edinburgh, 1955) ch. 6.
11. See K.H. Jackson on the mormaer, in *The Gaelic Notes in the Book of Deer* (Cambridge, 1972) pp. 102-10.
12. The remark is made by Marianus Scottus and is borrowed from Florence of Worcester.
13. A.O. Anderson, op. cit., pp. 472-4.
14. For this stone, see J. Romilly Allen and J. Anderson, op. cit., vol. III, pp. 149-51.
15. G.W.S. Barrow, *The Kingdom of the Scots* (London, 1973) ch. 1; Robert

A. Dodgshon, *Land and Society in Early Scotland* (Edinburgh, 1981) ch. 3.

16. G. Whittington and J.A. Soulesby, 'A preliminary report on an investigation into pit-placenames', *Scottish Geographical Magazine*, lxxxiv (1968) pp. 117-25.
17. Kathleen Hughes, *Celtic Britain in the Middle Ages* (Woodbridge, 1980) ch. 2.
18. *Andrea Scotis dvx esto compatriotis*. Discussed in G.W.S. Barrow, *Robert the Bruce and the Community of the Realm of Scotland* (Edinburgh, 1976) pp. 24-5.

## 11. Myths of the Dark Ages *Janet L. Nelson*

1. The distinction is illuminated, for the modern period, by the papers in E. Hobsbawm and T. Ranger (eds) *The Invention of Tradition* (Cambridge, 1983). E. Leach, *Levi-Strauss* (London, 1970) provides an excellent introduction to the foremost anthropological student of myth, and D. Sperber, *Rethinking Symbolism* (Cambridge, 1975) is a penetrating (and entertaining) critique.
2. For examples of such medieval myths, see S. Reynolds, 'Medieval *Origines Gentium* and the Community of the Realm', *History*, LXVIII (1983) pp. 375-90, and D. Dumville, 'Kingship, genealogies and regnal lists', in P.H. Sawyer and I.N. Wood (eds) *Early Medieval Kingship* (Leeds, 1977) pp. 72-104.
3. Translated by L. Thorpe, *The History of the Kings of Britain* (Harmondsworth, 1966).
4. R.S. Loomis (ed.) *Arthurian Literature in the Middle Ages* (Oxford, 1959); Mark Girouard, *The Return to Camelot: Chivalry and the English Gentleman* (New Haven and London, 1981).
5. H.C. Butterfield, *Magna Carta in the Historiography of the Sixteenth and Seventeenth Centuries* (Reading, 1969).
6. H.C. Butterfield, *The Whig Interpretation of History* (London, 1931); and especially C. Hill, 'The Norman Yoke', in his *Puritanism and Revolution* (London, 1958) pp. 50-122.
7. Girouard, op. cit., ch. 8.
8. Sir John Spelman, *Life of Alfred the Great*, written in 1643, published posthumously in 1678.
9. The Jubilee Edition of *The Whole Works of King Alfred the Great*, ed. J.A. Giles (London, 1858).
10. Thomas Hughes, *Alfred the Great* (London, 1871).
11. Alfred Bowker (ed.) *The King Alfred Millenary. A Record of the Proceedings of the National Commemoration* (London, 1902). These celebrations took place in 1901 because of the widely held but mistaken belief that Alfred had died in 901.
12. H.R. Loyn, *Anglo-Saxon England and the Norman Conquest* (London, 1962) pp. 199-223; P. Wormald, 'The Ninth Century', in J. Campbell (ed.) *The Anglo-Saxons* (Oxford, 1982) p. 142.

13. C. Arnold, 'Wealth and social structure', in P. Rahtz, T. Dickinson and L. Watts (eds) *Anglo-Saxon Cemeteries* (Oxford: British Archaeological Reports, British Series 82, 1980) pp. 81-142; see also Chapter 3.
14. *Maxims 1*, translated by T.A. Shippey, *Poems of Wisdom and Learning in Old English* (Cambridge, 1976).
15. G. Beresford, 'Goltho Manor, Lincolnshire: the buildings and their surrounding defences *c.* 850-1150', in R.A. Brown (ed.) *Proceedings of the Fourth Battle Conference 1981* (Woodbridge, 1982) pp. 13-36.
16. D. Pelteret, 'Slave raiding and slave trading in early England', *Anglo-Saxon England*, IX (1981) pp. 99-114.
17. D. Whitelock (ed.) *English Historical Documents, c.500-1042*, vol. I (second, revised edition, London, 1979) p. 468.
18. P.H. Sawyer, *From Roman Britain to Norman England* (London, 1978) pp. 168-78; see also Chapter 9.
19. A. Harding, *The Law-Courts of Medieval England* (London, 1973); J. Campbell (ed.) op. cit., p. 244.
20. P. Wormald, 'The uses of literacy in Anglo-Saxon England and its neighbours', *Transactions of the Royal Society*, fifth series, XXVII (1977) pp. 95-114, and M.T. Clanchy, *From Memory to Written Record* (London, 1979) pp. 12-17, offer excellent discussions of the problem of Anglo-Saxon literacy in a broader context. Both argue for only very restricted literacy in that period, but I follow S. Keynes, *The Diplomas of King Æthelred 'the Unready' 978-1016* (Cambridge, 1980) pp. 134-53, in thinking this view over-pessimistic.
21. M.A. Meyer, 'Land, charters and the legal position of Anglo-Saxon women', in B. Kanner (ed.) *The Women of England from Anglo Saxon Times to the Present* (London, 1980) pp. 57-82.
22. D. Whitelock (ed.) *The Will of Æthelgifu* (Oxford, 1968).
23. D. Hill, *An Atlas of Anglo-Saxon England* (Oxford, 1981), maps, 2:12 to 2:25, pp. 126-32.
24. A good way to verify this is to read the translations in M. Swanton, *Anglo-Saxon Prose* (London, 1975) and S.A.J. Bradley, *Anglo-Saxon Poetry* (London, 1982).
25. M. Wood, *The Dark Ages* (London, 1982) is a first-rate introduction to Alfred's reign. See also the invaluable collection of evidence in *Alfred the Great. Asser's 'Life of King Alfred' and Other Contemporary Sources*, translated with introduction and notes by S. Keynes and M. Lapidge (Harmondsworth, 1983).
26. J.L. Nelson, 'The problem of King Alfred's royal anointing', *Journal of Ecclesiastical History*, XVIII (1967) pp. 145-63; R.H.C. Davis, 'Alfred the Great: Propaganda and Truth', *History*, LVI (1971) pp. 169-82; P. Wormald, 'Bede, the Bretwaldas and the Origins of the gens Anglorum' in P. Wormald (ed.) *Ideal and Reality. Studies in Anglo-Saxon and Frankish History presented to J.M. Wallace-Hadrill* (Oxford, 1983) pp. 99-129.
27. Hobbes, *Behemoth* (1679), quoted in C. Hill, 'The Norman Yoke', op. cit., p. 55.

## 12. The Feudal Kingdoms of Europe *Philip Dixon*

1. P. Lasko, *The Kingdom of the Franks* (London, 1971) pp. 42-5; 63-70.
2. D. Bullough, *The Age of Charlemagne* (London, 1973) pp. 149, 166.
3. P. Grierson, 'Charlemagne and the Carolingian Achievement' in D. Talbot-Rice (ed.) *The Dark Ages* (London, 1965) especially pp. 295-8.
4. D. Bullough, 'The Empire under the Ottonians' in D. Talbot-Rice, op. cit., especially pp. 318-22.
5. D. Bates, *Normandy before 1066* (London, 1982) pp. 15-20.
6. R.A. Brown, *Origins of English Feudalism* (London, 1973) pp. 21-32.
7. ibid., p. 26.
8. R.A. Brown, *English Castles* (London, 1976) pp. 20-30; M. de Bouard, 'De L'Aula au Donjon'. *Archéologie Médiévale* III/IV (1973-4) pp. 124-6.
9. D. Bates, op. cit., note 5, pp. 124-6.
10. L. Musset, 'La renaissance urbane de Xe et XIe siècles dans l'Ouest de France' in *Etudes de Civilisation Médiévale* (Poitiers, 1974).
11. R.A. Brown, op. cit., note 8, p. 57.
12. B.K. Davidson, 'Origins of the Castle in England', *Archaeological Journal* CXXIV (1967) pp. 202-11; R.A. Brown, 'An Historian's Approach to the Origins of the Castle in England' *Archaeological Journal* CXXVI (1969) pp. 131-48, and a reply by B.K. Davidson, ibid., pp. 146-8.
13. F.M. Stenton, *Anglo-Saxon England* (Oxford, 1965) pp. 406-11.
14. P.H. Sawyer, *From Roman Britain to Norman England* (London, 1978) pp. 117-31.
15. D. Bates, op. cit., note 5, pp. 174-6.
16. G.N. Garmonsway (ed.) *The Anglo-Saxon Chronicle* (London, 1962) p. 219.
17. D. Bates, op. cit., note 5, pp. 180-2.

# Notes on Contributors

WENDY DAVIES is Reader in History at the University of London. She has published articles on early medieval history and is the author of three books: *An Early Welsh Microcosm* (1978); *The Llandaff Charters* (1982); and *Wales in the Early Middle Ages* (1982). Her current research is focused on an investigation of village society in ninth century Brittany.

PHILIP DIXON is a Lecturer in Archaeology at the University of Nottingham. He is the author of *Barbarian Europe* (1976), and has directed excavations on medieval sites, including Greenwich Palace, London. He is at present engaged on the sixteenth year of digging on the Neolithic, Iron Age and Dark Age fortress at Crickley Hill, Gloucestershire. He is also Honorary Secretary of the Council for British Archaeology.

A.A.M. DUNCAN is Professor of Scottish History and Literature at the University of Glasgow. He is presently completing an edition of the Charters of Robert I of Scotland. His books include *Scotland: the Making of the Kingdom* (1975) and he edited and revised, W. Croft Dickinson *Scotland from Earliest Times to 1603* (1977). He is also a member of the Royal Commission on the Ancient and Historical Monuments of Scotland.

RICHARD HODGES is Lecturer in Archaeology and Pre-History at the University of Sheffield. He has excavated in Britain and Italy, and is now excavating a Carolingian monastery in southern Italy. His books include *The Hamwih Pottery* (1981); *Dark Age Economics: the Origins of Towns and Trade AD600-1000* (1982); and with D. Whitehouse, *Mohammed, Charlemagne and the Origins of Europe* (1983).

JANET L. NELSON is Lecturer in History at King's College, London. She has published articles on the theory and practice of early medieval kingship and is currently working on the reign of the ninth century Carolingian king, Charles the Bald.

LIAM DE PAOR is Lecturer in History at University College, Dublin. He has worked on many excavations, both in Ireland and on the Continent. He is an experienced broadcaster on many subjects, and his books include *Divided Ulster* (1971), and (with M. de Paor) *Early Christian Ireland* (1978).

KLAVS RANDSBORG is Reader in Pre-Historic Archaeology at the University of Copenhagen. His research is concentrated on the Neolithic period, the Bronze Age and the first millenium AD. His most recent publication is *The Viking Age in Denmark* (1980), and he is presently engaged in studies of the Roman and post-Roman period in Denmark.

LESLEY M. SMITH, the editor, studied history at the University of St Andrews and Brasenose College, Oxford. She now works as a researcher for London Weekend Television. She has edited (with Geoffrey Parker) *The General Crisis of the Seventeenth Century* (1978) and is currently researching a book on the history of Britain during the Interregnum.

ALFRED P. SMYTH is Senior Lecturer in History at the University of Kent in Canterbury. He is a specialist in Viking and Celtic history. His books include *Scandinavian Kings in the British Isles* (1977); *Scandinavian York and Dublin: the History and Archaeology of Two Related Viking Kingdoms* (2 vols, 1975 and 1979); and *Celtic Leinster: Towards a Historical Geography of Early Irish Civilisation* (1982). He also broadcasts regularly on the radio on historical topics.

PAULINE STAFFORD is Senior Lecturer in History in the Department of Humanities, Huddersfield Polytechnic. She has written a number of articles on the tenth and eleventh centuries and is the author of *Queens, Concubines and Dowagers: the King's Wife in the Early Middle Ages* (1983), and *The East Midlands in the Early Middle Ages* (1984).

MALCOLM TODD is Professor of Archaeology at the University of Exeter. He was educated at the University of Wales and Brasenose College, Oxford, and subsequently taught (first as Lecturer, then as Reader) at the University of Nottingham. His books include *Everyday Life of the Barbarians* (1972); *The Northern Barbarians* (1975); and *Roman Britain 55BC-AD400* (1981).

PATRICK WORMALD is Lecturer in Medieval History at the University of Glasgow, and a Fellow of All Souls College, Oxford. He works on early English history in its continental and Celtic setting, was co-author of *The Anglo-Saxons* (ed. J. Campbell) and edited *Ideal and Reality in Frankish and Anglo-Saxon Kingship* (1983). His book on *Kingship and the Making of Law in England: from Alfred to Henry I* is forthcoming.

# Index

Aethelbald, king of Mercia 60
Aethelbert, king of Kent 56, 84-5
Aetius, Roman general 11
Agriculture 39-40, 98
Aidan, Christian monk 86-7
Alaric, leader of the Goths 10
  invasion of Italy by 10
  sack of Rome by 10
Alfred the Great, king of Wessex 53, 108-11, 114, 120, 147-50, 156-8, 168
Althaulf, leader of the Goths 19
  marriage to Galla Placida 19
Anglo-Saxons
  administration of 167-8
  art and craft of 87-8, 150
  coinage of 58-9, 157-8
  dynasties of 44
  graves of 43-4, 150
  kingdoms of 49-62 *passim*, and see *Kingdoms*
  kingship and 44, 47, 51-62
  language and literacy 163-4
  later rule of 125
  laws of 56, 153
  law courts of 153-4
  literature of 157-8
  migrations of 35-47 *passim* and see *migrations*
  myth of freedom of 146-7, 150
  myth of independence of 147, 150
  place-names of 44
  and religion 44, 78, 82
  settlement of 42-3, 80
  society of 37, 56-7, 150-4
  and taxation 57-8
  and women 154-5
*Anglo-Saxon Chronicle* 30, 33, 42, 60-1, 91, 94, 105-6, 114
Angus, over-king of the Picts 134-5
Arles, kingdom of 10-11
Art 87, 120, 131, 150
Arthur, king of Britain 145-6, 150
Athelstan, king of England 114-5
Attila, king of the Huns 11

barbarians 8
  border raids of 9
  burials of 16-17
  as mercenaries 32
  metalwork of 18
  migrations of 17-18, 39
  population increase of 16-17
  raids 21-2, 27-8, 30
  as settlers 19, 30, 32
  sophistication of 15
  tribes of 35

Bede, the Venerable, Christian monk 32, 35, 44, 46, 49, 51, 57, 59-60, 62, 83, 88-9, 105, 131
*Beowulf* 53, 57-60
Biscop, Benedict, Christian monk 88-9
Book of Deer 142
Book of Kells 141
*Bretwalda* 60
Britain, geography of 65
British society 72
  family life in 73-4

Canute, Danish and English king, 102, 119-20, 125, 139, 151, 154, 168
  sister of 150
Celts 35, 47
  chieftains of 38
  church of 46
  kings of 37-8, 46
  influence of British society of 32
  migration of 45-6
  raids of 45-6

society of 36-8, 46
Cenwulf, king of Mercia 52
Christianity 44, 77-90 *passim*, 127
coming of 47, 49, 61
*ecclesia Anglorum* 61
influence on society of 75
and kingship 127-9
missionaries 61
and pagan migrants 44-5
and Picts and Scots 142-3
spread of 75
and trade 44
churches 70
coinage 31-2, 52, 58-9, 111-12, 125, 126, 141, 167
Constantine, leader of dissident Romans 10, 22-3, 28

Danes 91-103 *passim*, 126, and see *Vikings*
agriculture of 98
expulsion from England of 102
farms of 95-6, 98
fortresses of 100-1
houses of 97
late society of 97-8
raids of 95, 101-2
and religion 97
settlement of 120-2
towns of 97, 101
Danegeld 126
Dubh, king of Scots 137-40

Eadred, king of Wessex and England 117
ealdormen 122, 125, 126-7, 168
Easter, controversy over 87-8
Edgar, king of England 117-18, 122-3, 125, 126
coronation of 127-9
Edmund St, king of East Anglia 109, 111
Edward the Confessor, king of England 129, 170-1
Egbert, king of Wessex 53, 60
England
administration of 122-9 *passim*
division of 117-20, 122
kingdom of 117-29 *passim*
unity of 127
Eric Bloodaxe, king of Norway 115, 117

Ethelred the Unready, king of England 119-20, 122-3, 125-6, 168
lawcode of 126

Feudal kingdoms 159-171 *passim*
feudalism 164-7
and military service 165-7
fiefs 164, 166-7, 168
Franks 10, 11, 19, 61, 82, 159, 167
kingdom of 159-64

Geoffrey of Monmouth, historian 145-6
Germanic peoples 37, 47
chiefs and kings of 38, 47
Gildas 30, 33
Gododdin, early Welsh poem 63-4
Goths 9, 11, 28
Gregory the Great, pope 49, 61, 83-4, 158
Guthrum 110-11

Harald, king of Danes 98-100
Harold Godwinsson, king of England 159, 167-8
defeat at Hastings 159
Huns 9
invasion of western Empire by 11
hundreds 124
hundred courts 153

Innes, Cosmo 3
Iona 75, 82, 105, 108, 131, 132, 142, 143
Irish 66-7
Christian communities 80
Christian mission to 77-8
Ivar the Boneless, king of Danes 106-7, 109, 111, 114

Kemble, John 2-3
Kenneth, king of Picts and Scots 135-6, 143
Kingdoms 68-70
Anglo-Saxon 49-62 *passim*
East Anglia 50-1, 52, 59, 111, 124
Mercia 50-3, 59, 124
Northumbria 50-1, 105
Wessex 50-1, 52, 61, 108, 109, 114, 117
British, development of 68-9
division of 136-7
feudal 158-171 *passim*

Pictish 69-70 and see *Picts*
Scottish, see *Scots*
Kingship, concept of 38, 44, 46, 47, 53-63 *passim*, 70, 90, 128, 161

language 65-6, 78, 89-90
Anglo-Saxon 153-4
Pictish and Scottish 132
'Lichfield Gospels' 72, 75-6
Lindisfarne 86, 105-6
sack of 91, 93
*Lindisfarne Gospels* 88-9

Malcolm II, king of Scotland 139
Malcolm III, (Canmore), king of Scotland 139
Maximus, Magnus, Roman commander 27-8
monasticism 78, 80-2
political effects of 127
monks 64
migrations 69, 71
Anglo-Saxon 40-2
Celtic 45-6, 66
Germanic 46

Norman Conquest 159, 171

Offa, king of Mercia 52-3, 61
coinage of 59
Offa's Dyke 52, 58, 117
Oswald, Archbishop of York 122, 128

Pelagius, English bishop 78
Penda, king of Mercia 51, 59
Picts 45, 63-76 *passim*, 77, 78, 82, 105,
art of 74, 131-2, 141
Sueno's Stone 140
kingdom of 131-42 *passim*
Pictish kings 155
Brude 82
place-names of 136
settlement of 141
society of 74
place-names 42, 131, 136, 164

Redwald, king of East Anglia 44
religion 77, see *Christianity*
of Anglo-Saxons 80, 83-4
of Danes 97
in Roman Britain 26-7, 44-5
Roman Empire
decline in institutions 25-6
Eastern part of Empire 15
recovery under Justinian 19
later fragmentation of 19-20
reasons for fall of 12-15
Roman rule of Britain 21, 23-7
and defence 27-8
end of 23, 28-33 *passim*, 35
Roman society 36
Roman towns 25-6, 30
Roman villas 24, 27, 65, 70
*Romanitas* 19
Ruthwell Cross 88-9

St Augustine, Benedictine monk 84-5
St Columba, Celtic monk 82, 90
*Life* of 74-5
St David 64
St Patrick 27
Scots 45, 63-76 *passim*, 105
commerce of 141
church of 142
kingdom of 131-42 *passim*
kings 137-40
and Shakespeare 137
and Vikings 134
Stilicho, Roman general 28
Sutton Hoo, burial ship 44, 56-9

taxation
and Anglo-Saxons 57-8
and British 72
and Picts 70
land tax of Ethelred 126
trade 33, 38, 39
and chiefs 38
and Christianity 44
between Normans and Anglo-Saxons 167
and Scots 141
tenth-century revival of 126
trade routes 92-4
and Vikings 92-5, 114
*Tribal Hidage* 58

Valens, Roman emperor 9
Vandals 11
Vikings 61, 91-103 *passim*, 105-16 *passim*, 163, 168
and agriculture 98
conquest of England (1013), 120
farms of 95-6, 98

fortresses of 98, 100-1
houses of 97
last invasions of 159
and Picts and Scots 134-5
political consequences of invasions 115-16
raids of 50-1, 94-5, 106, 163, 168
settlement of 94, 112-13, 157, 164
and trade 92-5, 114
Vortigern 32

Wapentakes 124
Whitby, meeting of 87-8
William the Conqueror, Duke of Normandy, King of England 159, 170-1
Wulfstan, Archbishop of York 114-15

Zosimos 22-3